Passing Over Easter

To my grandfathers,
Ferdinand Feher and Abraham Rosenvasser

Passing Over Easter
Constructing the Boundaries
of Messianic Judaism

Shoshanah Feher

ALTAMIRA
PRESS

A Division of Sage Publications, Inc.
Walnut Creek • London • New Delhi

For information contact:

AltaMira Press
A Division of Sage Publications, Inc.
1630 North Main Street, Suite 367
Walnut Creek, California 94596 U.S.A.
explore@altamira.sagepub.com

Sage Publications Ltd.
6 Bonhill Street
London EC2A 4PU United Kingdom

Sage Publications India Pvt. Ltd.
M-32 Market
Greater Kailash 1
New Delhi 110 048 India

PRINTED IN THE UNITED STATES OF AMERICA

Library of Congress Cataloging-in-Publication Data

Feher, Shoshanah.
    Passing over Easter : constructing the boundaries of Messianic Judaism / by Shoshanah Feher.
        p. cm.
    Includes bibliographical references and index.
    ISBN 0-7619-8952-8 (cloth). — ISBN 0-7619-8953-6 (pbk.)
    1. Jewish Christians—United States. I. Title.
BR158.F44 1998
289.9—dc21   97-45385
                                                CIP

98   99   00   01   02   03   04   05   06   07   10 9 8 7 6 5 4 3 2 1

Production and Editorial Services: David Featherstone
Editorial Management: Erik Hanson
Cover Design: Joanna Ebenstein

Contents

About the Author

Shoshanah Feher received her Ph.D. in sociology from the University of California, Santa Barbara, in 1995. She was a postdoctoral fellow with the New Ethnic and Immigrant Congregations Project, based at the University of Illinois at Chicago. Feher's published work spans the areas of ethnicity, gender, new religious movements, and Judaism in North America. She is currently on the research faculty of the School of Medicine at the University of California, Los Angeles, where she is conducting research on the interplay between quality of life, health, and religion in older women with breast cancer.

Acknowledgments

I had never heard of Messianic Jews until a few years ago, when Gordon Melton, the founder and director of the Institute for the Study of American Religion, mentioned them in conjunction with a book he was lending me from his extensive library. After it became clear that he was referring not to Hasidic Jews but to Jewish Christians, I responded (with what I later learned was a typical reaction) by saying disdainfully, "Oh, you mean Jews for Jesus?" But I was intrigued. Despite my interest in the topic, I found little information to satisfy my curiosity. Perhaps, I decided, the only way to understand what I took to be an oxymoron ("How can they be Christian *and* Jewish?") was to involve myself in such a community.

This book is the result of my active three-year involvement, from 1992 to 1995, at the Messianic congregation Adat haRuach. The project has been a community effort that has involved a large number of players, and came to fruition with the generous help of many people.

I am grateful to John Sutton, R. Stephen Warner, Denise Bielby, William Bielby, Roger Friedland, and Phillip Hammond, who aided in various developmental stages of this work. John Sutton continually encouraged me to problematize and analyze, pushing me to think at my outer limits. R. Stephen Warner guided me in the world of ethnography, ever present with advice, support, and encouragement.

I would like to thank the agencies that granted me funds to conduct this study: the National Science Foundation for a Doctoral Dissertation Research Improvement Grant; the Society for the Scientific Study of Religion for a research grant; the Religious Research Association for a Constant H. Jacquet

Research Award; and the University of California, Santa Barbara, for the Humanities/Social Sciences Research Grant and for a grant from the Department of Sociology.

Thanks also to Mitch Allen, publisher, and Erik Hanson, my editor, at AltaMira Press, and in particular to David Featherstone, for his careful and thoughtful editing of the text.

Many others have helped along the way as well. Val Jenness, Nancy Eiesland, Naomi Abrahams, Jan Salinger-McBride, and Penny Edgell Becker have been a source of personal and professional support throughout the project. Gordon Melton generously shared his ideas and his library and introduced me to the world of Messianic Judaism. Lynn Davidman, Debra Kaufman, and Melody Knutson read drafts of early chapters. Leon Zamosc, Hugh Mehan, Robert Sapolsky, and Marilyn Perrin influenced my professional career early on. Phillip Lucas and Mark Shibley were my church-hopping companions, and Martha McCaughey, Laura Grindstaff, and Francie Montell were my "cohort women" companions. Lynn and Aharon Gibor provided a home-away-from-home during my time in Santa Barbara.

I would also like to thank my father, George Feher, for passing on to me his enthusiasm for asking questions and seeking answers about the world around him. He has always stood behind me, instilled confidence, and passed on "tricks of the trade." I thank my sister, Paola Feher, and Geno Mecina, for all their support, particularly during my fieldwork. My mother, Elsa Feher, has been my pillar of strength and support for many years. She has been excited with me at the start of a new project and encouraging when the project seemed difficult. She has carefully and critically read more drafts of my work than I (and surely she) care to remember. Throughout it all, she has imparted precious nuggets of her philosophy of life. Finally, I am infinitely grateful to my partner, Geoff Sternlieb, for his unending support and unwavering faith in me. Most importantly, I thank him for always making me laugh and for seeing humor and promise at every turn.

In concluding, I would especially like to thank the community of Adat haRuach. They trusted me to tell their story as honestly as possible and without the judgment they encounter in the secular world. I hope I have done them justice. I also hope that the warmth, openness, and support they offered me are evident in these pages. In particular, I thank Rabbi Jason Slater, for allowing me to participate; the Northrops and the Reuttegers, for immediately incorporating me into their circles; and the Pierces, for taking me under their wing. I am especially grateful to Wiley and Abby for never losing patience with my ignorance, for teaching me the meaning of "edification," and for our friendship, which continues to develop.

Exodus and
Communion

"We are *mishpoche* [family], the family of the Lord. We are here together to relax and to fellowship. Good *Yom Tov* [Happy Holiday] and Happy Passover. Tonight we celebrate our freedom, just as Yshua [Jesus] taught his disciples." These remarks greeted almost seven hundred persons in the converted gymnasium of a nondenominational Christian fellowship.[1]

The Messianic rabbi who had greeted us stood on the stage. A trim man of forty with piercing blue eyes, Rabbi Jason wore a light brown suit, a tie, and a white *kippah* (skullcap). His wife stood at his side, her long, curly brown hair complemented by a suit in black and various shades of brown. The wall behind the couple was decorated with a large Israeli flag flanked by blue-and-white flags displaying Judaean lions. On the wall behind the flags, one could see the faint outline of the word *Jesus* painted in giant script, a clear indication to those arriving that, while everything looked Jewish, there was a definite Christian undertone. Large potted palms and ficus plants were on the stage, along with the guitars, clarinet, bass flute, and piccolo of the musicians who had played and sung while we entered the hall. In front of the rabbi and his wife was a table, covered by a white cloth, that held a pair of candlesticks and other objects needed for the evening service. The rabbi's wife placed a white lace scarf on her hair and said a blessing while lighting the two candles. Thus began the Passover Seder at Adat haRuach (Community of the Spirit).[2]

Several weeks earlier, I had told my family that I would not be celebrating Passover with them at home as usual but that, since I was in the midst of fieldwork, I intended to attend Adat haRuach's community Seder. My mother, always ready for a cultural adventure, said that if I couldn't celebrate with them, they would come and celebrate with me. By then, I had gotten used to many of the Messianic ways, and I was glad for the opportunity to see the Seder through new (Jewish) eyes as I monitored my family's reactions and explained to them what was happening at various points.[3]

THE SEDER CELEBRATION

When I arrived with my family, Abby ran out to greet me and to tell me that she had saved seats for us at the table at which she and Simon were sitting. As we walked toward our table, it was hard not to notice that the guests were in a festive mood and were dressed for the occasion. All the men wore *kippot* (skullcaps), and white *kippot* were provided at the entrance for those who did not bring their own. All of the decorations were blue and white, Israel's colors, even down to the blue-and-white cups, plastic place settings, and napkins on the round tables that packed the gymnasium. Each setting included a place with a piece of gefilte fish on a bed of lettuce. At the center of each table was an Israeli flag and a wreath of silk flowers and berries surrounded by traditional sesame-seed candies. An identifying table number was printed on a piece of laminated cardboard inside a Star of David. Each table also held the traditional Seder accoutrements: a shankbone, an egg, matzoh, sprigs of parsley, bottles of wine and grape juice, and bowls of saltwater, horseradish, and an apple-and-nut mixture.

While my parents and sister were a bit overwhelmed by the enthusiastic welcome they were receiving by people who were "thrilled to meet Shoshanah's family," they so far felt they were on relatively familiar territory. I say "relatively" only because none of us had ever attended a Seder for seven hundred people or, for that matter, a Seder outside a family home. That feeling of being on familiar territory changed as soon as Rabbi Jason began the dinner service. In describing what was on the table he said,

The strange foods we have before us remind us of spiritual lessons and remind us of where we came from. For example, the bitter herbs remind us of a bitter life, of physical slavery. Regardless of our past, we can all relate in some way, somehow. Through Yshua HaMashiach [Hebrew for "Jesus Christ," literally "Jesus the Messiah"], God has redeemed us, and that is why, for Believers, Passover takes on new meaning. Tonight we are reminded of the parting of the Red Sea, that it is God who parts and guides through difficult times.

Once an avid surfer, the rabbi could not resist an analogy: "Like a surfer coming out of the ocean, God has led us out of difficult times. Praise God for His work tonight." This informal allusion is characteristic of Rabbi Jason's casual style, a style that permeates his congregation.

Rabbi Jason then explained the traditional items laid out on each table. The *zeroah* (lamb shankbone) represents the means of redemption, the blood of the sacrifice, and the way in which Yshua haMashiach became the *Pesach* (Passover) sacrifice. The *baytzah* (roasted egg) represents the burnt offerings of the Temple period. The *maror* (bitter herbs—in this case, horseradish) represent the bitterness of slavery and the terrible bondage of the oppressed. At the Last Supper, the Messianic rabbi said, Yshua took a portion of the bitter herbs, told John that the person he gave it to was the one who would betray him, and handed it to Judas. The *charoset* (a sweet apple-and-nut mixture) is a reminder of the sweetness of the redemption. The *karpas* (green spring herbs—in this case, parsley) speaks of life.

The Messianic rabbi went on to explain the significance of the matzoh cover, the *matzoh tasch*, a linen pillowcase with three separate compartments. During the Seder, one piece of matzoh is placed in each compartment. He told us that, over the centuries, the rabbis have asked themselves, "What does this [three compartments in one case] mean?" "Well?" he queried, "Does it sound familiar to you?" As the congregants tittered, he continued,

It must mean the unity: three in one. It may remind us of our forefathers: Abraham, Isaac, and Jacob, or of the unity of the

household of Israel: the Cohens, the Levites, and the
commoners. For those of us who are Messianics, it makes
perfect sense to us. It is such a beautiful picture of God, isn't
it? Of the *Shema*, [the prayer proclaiming] that God is one.
More literally, God is a oneness, a unity, with plural names.
God is revealed as three persons: God, the Mashiach, and the
Holy Spirit. Each has a distinct role, but all are one. This
symbolism is so beautiful. But if you think this [the close
connection between the Jewish and Christian symbols] is
weird, it gets weirder.

Wrapping the three matzoh in the linen pouch and pointing to the middle
matzoh, Rabbi Jason declared that, in the Bible, leaven—and anything that is
fermented—represents sin.

During preparation it [the matzoh] is perforated, and it is
pierced and striped. Isaiah says that the Messiah will be
pierced through for our iniquities and will be striped. We
were healed by that Roman whip [that striped Yshua].

In other words, the matzoh has holes because it has been pierced. The stripes
are reminders of the stripes on Yshua's back from the whipping he suffered at
the hands of the Romans. To ensure that we realized that traditional matzoh—which "even" the mainstream Jewish community eats—is also pierced
and striped, Rabbi Jason said, "I remind you, this is not Messianic matzoh.
This is out of the Jewish caterer's stove."

Traditionally, unleavened bread was eaten to commemorate the Israelites' exodus from Egypt. They were so rushed that they could not wait for the
yeast to rise in the bread they were baking. As Rabbi Jason broke the middle
matzoh, the *afikomen*, he said,

Afikomen is a Greek word, and it gives us a clue about the
origins of the ceremony. Why is it not a Hebrew term? Why
not Aramaic? The Greek times were around the first century
and *afikomen* means "He will come again" [or, in another
interpretation "I will return"].

Rabbi Jason continued,

> This makes sense to us Messianic Believers, doesn't it? At
> this time, we wrap up the middle matzoh. After He was
> broken for our inequities, He was enshrouded. So do we
> now. He was hidden for a while and buried. He will come
> again. You Christians know about the Easter egg hunt. Well,
> tonight we'll do an *afikomen* hunt.

The symbolism of matzoh, Rabbi Jason stressed from the gymnasium stage,
is not just about housecleaning and ridding the house of leavening.[4] Matzoh
reminds us of our need for spiritual cleansing and repentance. Therefore,
whenever we eat a matzoh sandwich during Pesach, we are reminded of the
meaning of the holy day. Every time we long for a leavened cookie, we remember this spiritual truth.

Rabbi Jason noted that in the New Testament, which he calls the "New
Covenant," the Messiah compared himself with this bread when he celebrated
the Passover. The symbolism, the rabbi said, is clear: Matzoh is a symbol of
the sinless Yshua, and breaking the *afikomen* symbolizes the breaking of the
body of Yshua. By wrapping the *afikomen* in linen, we remember the wrapping Yshua's body in linen after the crucifixion. When the broken half of the
matzoh is placed under the pillow, Yshua's burial is reenacted. After the meal
is over, the pillow is removed, just as the stone of Yshua's tomb was removed
by the angel. Then the wrapped *afikomen* is taken out and unwrapped, signi-
fying the resurrection. For Believers, breaking the matzoh into small pieces
and eating them after the meal signifies the Believer feeding on Yshua, Bread
of Life. The rabbi referred us to Luke 19, the chapter that recounts how Yshua
broke the matzoh and distributed the pieces in remembrance of him.

Rabbi Jason asked us, "Why do we, as Messianic Believers, celebrate
the Passover? Because in Exodus 12 God says we must remember." He went
on to describe the Passover as a sacrifice, and told how the sacrificial lamb,
unblemished and spotless, was selected carefully. Blood from this sacrificial
animal was sprinkled on the doorposts of Jewish homes to protect the marked
homes from the angel of death. The families accepted this means of protection by God, and were delivered from bondage as a result. For Messianic

Believers, the message is clear: God promises to pass over Believers with his judgment of death as long as they are willing to remain under his protection. Rabbi Jason believes that the prophetic fulfillment of Passover can be summed up best by the word *redemption*; slaying the lamb at Passover foreshadowed the greater redemption found in "God's appointed lamb, the Messiah."

The rabbi told the Messianic Believers that they celebrated Passover not only to commemorate the affliction and redemption in Egypt, but also to remind them of Yshua's redemption and affliction "for you." He added,

> It is very important to remember this time of year, which is very important for Messianic Jews and Gentiles. This is a special ceremony to remember the truth. Visitors, we're glad you had the nerve to come join us. We don't want to put you on the spot, so this can mean just the *afikomen* [in the traditional sense] to you. But we'll all partake together. It's what is in your hearts that matters. If you are a Believer and are redeemed, you can partake in the full meaning. If not, partake and thank God for the redemption of Egypt. But ask yourself: Why not receive the full redemption of God? You may not be a Believer, but the spirit of God may have tugged at your heart [tonight]. If you're a Jew and feel you can't turn on your people, we're here to tell you, it's the fulfillment of your Judaism. The question, the Jewish question, is "Who is the Messiah?" Let us bow our heads and pray.

We closed our eyes and prayed. During this interlude, three "new sheep" (converts) came up to the altar, having accepted Yshua into their hearts. Rabbi Jason asked us to "Give the Lord an offering of praise!" Everyone clapped enthusiastically, welcoming the new Believers.

Rabbi Jason led the service, using the Messianic Passover Hagaddah. In Hebrew, the term *Hagaddah* means "a telling." It is the name of the book used by one generation to tell the Passover story to the next generation. The edition of the Hagaddah used at Adat haRuach's Seder, produced by Lederer Messianic Ministries, contains most of the traditional Jewish readings as well as relevant New Covenant passages and explanations.

During the catered dinner, the congregants drank the traditional four cups of wine, dipped the herbs, ate the *charoset* (almost as good as mom's, my sister pointed out), and heard the age-old story of the Israelites' redemption from bondage. The children sang the traditional four questions, and everyone sang the traditional songs to traditional melodies. Some songs included new verses, however. For example, to the traditional verses of *Dayenu,*

> *Elu Elu, hotzianu mi Mitzrayim, dayenu!*
> *Elu, Elu natan lanu et ha Torah, dayenu!*
> Had he but taken us out of Egypt (and nothing more), it
> would have been sufficient!
> Had he but given us the Torah (and nothing more), it would
> have been sufficient!

was added a new final verse:

> *Elu Elu natan lanu et Yshua, dayenu!*
> Had he but given us Yshua (and nothing more), it would
> have been sufficient!

Near the end of the Seder, Rabbi Jason reminded us,

> There will come a time—some day, some year—when we
> will all call out *Baruch haba b'shem Adonai*! [Blessed is He
> who comes in the name of the Lord, (Matthew 23:37–39)],
> Yshua is the Messiah. He sent for us [Jews] and all Gentiles;
> the same Yshua we're told not to read about, not to say out
> loud. And the Gentiles will come this way, will be grafted in.
> Funny how two thousand years has turned it around. And
> many, most of us, are from Jewish backgrounds and have
> said *Baruch H'abba* [Blessed be the Father]. It is a taste of
> what will happen in all Seders of all nations. May it come
> soon when all Israel will say, "Welcome, praised be He."

At the end of the service, Rabbi Jason and two other men picked up their instruments. Beside them, two women dressed in blue and white sang and clapped as they swayed to the tunes. At the foot of the stage, many participants joined enthusiastically in circle dances reminiscent of Israeli dances. As we departed, my parents and sister were exhausted from trying to keep up with a new language and the new approach to an old tradition.

THE SEDER AS METAPHOR

The Seder serves as a metaphor for Messianic Judaism in general and Adat haRuach in particular because Passover is the most important holiday celebration of the congregation and therefore attracts the largest number of people. The Seder at Adat haRuach, like Messianic Judaism, attempts to bridge Christian and traditional Jewish ideologies. It shows the Jewishness of Jesus's roots and demonstrates how, as Believers in Jesus, Jews can maintain the traditional ritual of their childhood. Congregants have done this by recoding Jewish ritual and infusing it with Christian meaning. Some congregants elsewhere take communion every Sunday or once a month, but at Adat haRuach, communion is received once a year, at Passover. The Messianic movement has eliminated the elements of Christian worship that cannot be directly linked to their Jewish roots. Communion is therefore associated with Passover, since the Eucharist originated during Yshua's Last Supper, held at Passover. In this way, Passover is given a new, Yshua-centered meaning.

Passover is only one example of the constant decoding and recoding of Jewish ritual by Messianic Judaism. This decoding and recoding—the infusion of Jewish ritual and cultural norms with Christian symbolism and, to a lesser extent, the infusion of Christianity with Jewish symbolism—is a central theme of this book. This active form of culture, which continuously recreates and redefines Jewish ritual in Christian terms—is what binds the community of Messianics. Perhaps the only predictable feature of the community's cultural/religious norms is its unpredictability. I believe that Messianic Judaism derives strength from this consistent inconsistency. By *consistent inconsistency* I mean that the inconsistency is itself predictable, that Messianic Judaism has the latitude to do the culture work necessary to negotiate its positions. Adherents are welcome, even encouraged, to negotiate each and every rite, ritual, ceremony, and cultural norm with a "Messianic vision." When this is contrasted with the dogmatic denial of Jesus's Jewish roots by both mainstream Jews and Christians, one appreciates why Messianic adherents find Messianic Judaism such an attractive alternative.

Over the past few decades, Messianic Judaism has grown slowly but steadily into a bounded community. Messianic Jews[5] insist on the legitimacy of their hybrid beliefs, but the mainstream Jewish community feels that Messianic Judaism has transgressed the most important of traditional Jewish boundaries, the line dividing Jew from Christian. By adopting Christianity, Messianic Jews, in Douglas's (1966) language, have made the situation "messy." By refusing to recognize the Jewish/Christian boundary, they have put things out of order, a situation that creates great discomfort among normative Jews. Groups whose boundaries are threatened in this way typically respond by attempting to reestablish the challenged order and to reaffirm the boundary lines. Thus, in response to the threat by Messianic Judaism, the Jewish community has sought to clarify the boundary between Jewish and Gentile cultures. These responses alert community members to the interests they share and draw attention to those values that constitute the symbolic core of the community.

While Messianic Judaism identifies with its Jewish and Christian parent communities, it borrows elements from both and simultaneously breaks away from them to form its own new and separate community. Most Messianic members grew up in the Jewish community, yet the Jewish community does not regard them as members. Messianic Judaism also fails to fit neatly into the Christian community because of its strong ethnic identity and the values and norms associated with being Jewish. It is a community of overlaps: Jews appropriating Christian imagery, Christians appropriating Jewish culture.

There are many different lenses through which Messianic Judaism can be studied and interpreted. For a perspective, for example, on how Evangelicals—or other Christians—perceive Messianic Judaism, see *Christianity Today* 1988; Sidey 1990; Rausch 1982a, 1982b; Stokes 1994. My lens, however, is decidedly that of a normative Jew. My interest in Jewish Christians grew in large part from a personal desire to understand more about Jewish identity. In my own life, social factors had more bearing on my development as a Jew than faith or belief. I was brought up in a nonobservant home, where religious ritual was minimal and synagogue attendance rare. Nevertheless, Jewish cultural identity was nurtured and fostered. The daughter of a Holocaust survivor, I wondered how other Jews could abandon their heritage, their ancestors, or the memory of those who had been killed during the Holocaust?

Examining Jewish identity calls into question what it means to be a Jew and what Judaism is about. For practicing religious Jews, distinctions between ethnicity and religion are not so crucial because of their strong ties with both. For acculturated or assimilated Jews, the issues become more complex. In this latter group, the sense of Jewish identity may be very strong, yet independent of whether one attends services or believes in God (Dolgin 1977; Herman 1989; Schnapper 1983; Shibutani 1965).

The interweaving of nationhood with religiosity that characterizes Judaism makes it very difficult to discuss this "total religion" (Goffman 1959) in the same way as many other Western religions (Schnapper 1983; Herman 1977). Perhaps one way to understand Jewish identity is to consider it as both an ethnic and a spiritual identity. Often both of these identities are Jewish; in some cases, however, the ethnic identity is Jewish but the spiritual identity is not. Ethnic Jewish identities can be explained through childhood socialization; but many of the spiritual identities, because they emerge in adulthood, are based on reference groups developed later (Fein 1988; Herman 1989; Neusner 1981; Shibutani 1965).

How does a "subgroup" of American Judaism maintain its Jewish identity while simultaneously adding another spiritual identity, that of Christianity? The study of the Messianic movement has implications for understanding issues of identity; it also contributes to understanding issues of identity and boundaries on a larger scale. Identity, after all, is a "typified self at a stage in the life course situated in a context of organized social relations" (Weigert et al. 1986:53).

Lynn Davidman (1991), in her study of women that return to Jewish Orthodoxy, deals with the issue that identity plays in these women's decisions to return. They garner a sense of who they are by being a part of a religious tradition whose people reach far into the past as well as into the future. Being a part of a community with far-reaching roots gives the woman a sense of stability, continuity, and community. Danzger (1989) found similar narratives among men and women who returned to an Orthodox expression of their Judaism. Their concern was with the historical roots of their "people" as well as with their connections to their parents and grandparents. Maintaining these social ties was an important aspect of their search for meaning.

Issues of religious identity are not only important in Judaism, but also in conservative Christian groups. Ammerman (1987), in her ethnography of Fundamentalism, tells how being saved is the most important aspect of a Fundamentalist's identity; it provides assurance of the future and allows the individual a place of worship in the local church. Writing about an Evangelical church, Warner (1988) discusses how the group's religious identity promotes solidarity. This cohesiveness engenders the social strength that he witnessed on his first foray into the field; the way the Evangelicals used the term *Christian* made it clear to him that Christian was an achieved identity— one that took work and effort to maintain. McGuire (1982) and Neitz (1987) write that the Charismatic Catholic movement provides norms to combat the loss of identity and meaning that is common in the secular world.[6] The way Charismatic Catholics filter and give meaning to the situations and events in their lives confirms their Christian identity.

The issue of identity among Messianic Judaism has a similar ring to that of Charismatic Catholics. Both Neitz (1987) and McGuire (1982) talk about their respondents as feeling very Catholic both before and after they become Charismatic. Like Messianic Jews, Charismatics Catholics come to reinterpret their rituals and view the conventional ritual as an enrichment to their current practice; they interpret their conversion as continuous with their former belief system (Neitz 1987). Like Charismatics (McGuire 1982), Messianic Believers' new religious identity has enabled them to consolidate elements of both former identities into a new and "better" self. Messianics are active participants in the process of their identity formation. They assemble their identity by drawing on their repertoire of institutionally monitored cultural symbols (see Nagel 1994; Swidler 1986).

In this book, I discuss how a new religious movement creates, maintains, and reproduces itself. I analyze how its identity is shaped through language, ritual, history, boundaries, and gender and explore the issues facing a community that manages two identities considered mutually exclusive and historically incompatible. In chapter 2, I examine the relationship between Messianic Judaism and its Jewish parent community, and I take a close look at that the Jewish community's response to a group that transgresses boundaries by crossing over a "Christian line." Chapter 3 examines the historical development of Messianic Judaism and the move from a Christian-centered to an increasingly Judaized movement. In chapter 4, I paint a picture of who joins a Messianic congregation and why; in chapter 5, I explain how the Messianic community creates and dissolves boundaries with regard to its Evangelical and Jewish parent communities.[7] Chapter 6 explores Messianic Believers' enactment of boundaries through their use of ritual. In chapter 7, I examine gender expectations as a continuous negotiation of norms and community building. In the final chapter I discuss the implications for the future of the Messianic community and how, in attempting to break down walls between Jew and Gentile, Messianic Believers erect barriers of their own.

Chapter 2

Boundaries, Threats, and Assimilation

The American Jewish Community in Relation to Messianic Judaism

The Jewish community is most disturbed by the Messianics' insistence on maintaining their Jewish identity. Those who convert from Judaism to Christianity may be upsetting because they leave the fold, but Messianic Jews straddle the cultures and cause havoc by confusing the boundaries and mixing classifications. This is not only true of Messianic Jews, but of all Jews who become Christian and continue to consider themselves Jews. Included in this category are Hebrew Christians, which differ from Messianic Jews not in their identification as Jews, but in the extent to which they integrate Judaism into their religious life. Jews for Jesus, perhaps the most prominent of the Hebrew Christian groups, uses considerably less Jewish ritual than Messianic Judaism, and its members worship in established Christian churches rather than in their own congregations.[1]

Faced with this contamination of classifications, the Jewish community has had to rethink the meaning of being Jewish and where it draws its boundaries. In dealing with such issues, the Jewish community has mobilized itself and has developed anticult groups. It has made clear that Messianic Jews, like other Jews who join new religious movements, are marginalized; but there is still hope they can be brought back inside the boundary lines. The option of return is of utmost importance for a community that actively remembers the days when its members were forcibly removed. In particular, it is felt that Messianic Jews must be retrieved not only because they have left Judaism but because they have fled to the dominant culture, which has been at odds with the Jewish community for two thousand years.

In the United States, the contemporary Jewish community is so diverse that it is difficult to map it, or even to define it, accurately. In earlier generations in Europe, the confines of *shtetl* (Yiddish for "small village") life and widespread anti-Jewish sentiment kept Jews together and marked a clear boundary between Jews and Gentiles. Since the early twentieth century, however, increased mobility and the near-model assimilation of American Jews have blurred this line. In this chapter, to clarify how the American Jewish community defines itself, I focus on the Jewish community of Los Angeles, a community considered to be "The West Coast headquarters of the great countrywide Jewish unsteadiness" (Elazar 1976:252), and concentrate on that community's response to Messianic Judaism and the threat it represents to Jewish identity.

The Los Angeles Jewish community, like the American Jewish community in general, is marked by its diversity; it encompasses Ashkenazic, Sephardic, Orthodox, Conservative, Reform, Reconstructionist, and unaffiliated Jews, to name but a few divisions. The largest Jewish community in the western United States, it consists of well over a half-million people (Kosmin and Scheckner 1992). Because of its size, Los Angeles serves as the West Coast headquarters of many national Jewish groups. Daniel Elazar notes that because of this community's network of institutions, it is more closely knit than any other large Jewish community. He adds (1976:252) that Los Angeles is one of the "Jewish frontiers of the contemporary world, where openness to innovation has consistently been greater than in more established regions." This is in part because it was settled by American-born Jews who came with the organizational skills characteristic of American culture. Also because of its geography, the Los Angeles community is widespread; it never depended on a compact inner city.

According to Elazar, contemporary American Jewry is based on noncentralized decision making. The community, he claims, can best be understood as a mosaic, "a multidimensional matrix of institutions and organizations that interact with each other and [are] bound by shared patterns of culture, with some overlap of membership and of leadership" (1976:77). This mosaic is overlaid by a series of uneven concentric circles that radiate outward from a core of committed Jews toward areas of "vague Jewishness" on the fringes. Elazar describes the boundaries between the circles as fluid, with considerable movement in and out. Indeed, he states that

> what characterizes a society composed of concentric circles is precisely the fact that there are no boundaries; what holds people within it is the pull of its central core, particularly as its outer edges become increasingly blurred. Perhaps the most appropriate image for this is a magnet . . . a magnet at the core pulls those who contain . . . the iron filings of Judaism closer to the center, more or less according to the degree of their iron (i.e., Jewish) content. (1976:77)

By understanding how these circles work, one can see how the American Jewish community defines itself and whether there is consensus about the location of the outer "fringe," the ultimate boundary. To map out the Jewish community, we must learn the relative positions of the organizations that support, maintain, and reproduce American Jewry. This knowledge in turn will help us to understand the place of Messianic Judaism in relation to the mainstream community.

To address this question, I spoke with the official representatives of several national Jewish organizations in Los Angeles.[2] These organizations span a variety of institutions, but all deal with issues relating to Jewish culture and community within the United States, as opposed to religious and congregational concerns, the State of Israel, or welfare. These organizations include the American Jewish Committee, the American Jewish Congress, the Anti-Defamation League of B'nai B'rith, the Jewish Community Relations Council (JCRC), Jews for Judaism, and the Cult Clinic of the Jewish Family Service.

To learn more fully and precisely who is considered a part of the Jewish community and to understand the criteria those who are included as Jews, I examined how the community responds to deviant religious expressions. I also examined the "stress points" of the Jewish community's boundaries by focusing on the community's perception of, and response to, Messianic Judaism. The Messianic movement is an ideal example of a perceived threat to Jewish community integrity because it meets with universal rejection—indeed, disdain—from the entire Los Angeles Jewish community.

BOUNDARIES OF THE LOS ANGELES COMMUNITY

The term *Jewish community* is used easily and often. What does it mean? Whom does it include and exclude? Despite the compact expression, it does not describe a monolith. The spokespeople whom I met represent the full spectrum of organized Jewry in the United States. Some, like Rabbi Gary Greenbaum of the American Jewish Committee, adhere to the most liberal of definitions of *Jewish Community*, that of David Ben-Gurion, the first president of Israel—the Jewish community is made up of anyone who identifies as a Jew. Others, like Rabbi Ben-Tzion Kravitz of Jews for Judaism, consider this a good nation-building policy but a poor definition of a religious community. He takes a staunch traditionalist viewpoint—if your mother is Jewish, so are you; if she is not, neither are you; if you are converting, only an Orthodox, *halachic* (done according to Jewish law) conversion will do.

A few of the organizational representatives spoke of an inclusive identity—the Jewish community exists by virtue of whom it includes—while others defined the community by excluding those not seen as Jewish. That is, they talk about what they are *not*. Some respondents referred to the valence—positive or negative—of identity, or rooted their definitions in the Holocaust and in persecution or anti-Semitism. Zionism, ethnicity, religious education, lifestyle, intermarriage, and assimilation or acculturation were additional defining parameters the spokespeople mentioned.

Perhaps the most inclusive view is held by Rabbi Laura Geller of the American Jewish Congress, who called on her feminist ideology to make sense of the question. She believes that the Jewish community is composed of everyone who has any kind of relationship to the Jewish community. Rabbi Geller pointed out that although she may not want to invite all of them to her home, or to her synagogue, they are nonetheless *amcha*, part of the Jewish people. In her words,

I think that one of the real gifts of feminism is to teach us
that the community of Israel includes everybody. . . .
Feminism says, "We're here, too; and it has to be addressed
to us, too." It makes you stop and say, "Well, who else is
really here but hasn't been addressed?" And among that
group of people [are] gays and lesbians, Jews who don't
have any money, children of divorce, people in
nontraditional families. All of the categories of Jews that you
know and that I know but that the Jewish community doesn't
know . . . I think that's one of feminism's great gifts; it
forces us to think very differently about God, Torah, and
Israel. Israel—meaning the Jewish people—is a whole
different phenomenon when you look at it through these
inclusive eyes.

Rabbi Geller regards Judaism as a large family with relatives one likes and
relatives one does not like, but a family nonetheless.

Instead of it being a family, Rabbi Abraham Cooper, spokesman for the
Simon Wiesenthal Center in Los Angeles, likens American Jewry to a nation.
In his view, being a part of the Jewish community is independent of any
formal relationship with the community.

If you are born in the United States [and] you never get a
passport, you don't get a Social Security card and you don't
use the social agencies, you're still a full-blooded American.
Right? Same kind of definition [for a Jew].

All of my interviewees said that they do not consider Messianics to be
part of the Jewish community. Rabbi Geller's "family" analogy seemed to
falter in the face of the Messianic question.

They [Messianics] are not Jews. They are people who are
trying to convert Jews. . . . I don't think they're really

relatives. I think they're people who are pretending to be
relatives and using their pretended relative status to trick the
rest of my family.

Similarly, Rabbi Greenbaum's liberal definition, whereby anyone who identifies as a Jew is a Jew, did not extend to Messianic Jews. When I mentioned
Messianic Jews to Rabbi Cooper, he invoked the Jewish collective experience over thousands of years.

> The fact remains that Christianity is another faith and
> Judaism is both a faith and a peoplehood . . . they [Hebrew
> Christians] were obviously initially not accepted by the
> mainstream Jewish world. They eventually started their own
> religion, didn't they?

Rabbi Cooper believes that when Jews identify with another faith, they cease
to be members of the Jewish community. He quickly differentiated, however,
between sincere soul searching and active proselytizing, and made clear that
Messianic Jews fall into the latter (insincere) category:

> I think there's a difference between someone who's
> searching for meaning in their life and maybe making
> mistakes along the line as opposed to someone who opens up
> a Jewish Messianic synagogue . . . and devotes his or her
> energies to trying to attract other Jews out of their faith into
> another faith community.

Rabbi Kravitz believes that Messianics have renounced their Jewish
identity. He explained,

> You're Jewish if you're born of a Jewish woman or convert.
> That ensures a special relationship, the covenant with God,
> and you're always under obligation to fulfill it. But if you
> don't, you can't have full membership in the community.

Kravitz quoted Moishe Rosen, founder of Jews for Jesus, who said, "Both my parents were Jewish; no one can take that away from me." Kravitz continued,

> He's right. No one can. And no one can take away that
> you're born Jewish, even if you convert. You will have
> always been Jewish, but that doesn't mean that you have a
> Jewish relationship with God.

He added, however, that even *no* relationship with God is better than a Messianic relationship, "After all, no one is an atheist in a foxhole."

All of these spokespersons believe that Jewish identity in the United States is threatened by acculturation. None of them uses Jewish observance or religiosity as a measure of "Jewishness," yet they unanimously condemn Messianic Judaism, whose members are Jewish in their knowledge and appreciation of Judaism in every aspect but religious doctrine.

STRADDLING THE FENCE: MESSIANIC JUDAISM AS A UNIQUE THREAT TO THE JEWISH COMMUNITY

The contemporary Jewish community in the United States is concerned more with internal relationships than with external boundaries. Today this community is "strong grid, weak group," in Mary Douglas's (1970) terms[3]—a collectivity of constituent subgroups or individuals. Steve Windmueller, director of the Los Angeles Jewish Community Relations Council (JCRC), spoke of the shift from group to grid in his own words when he acknowledged that the Jewish community is more narrowly defined now than in the past, saying, "That's because [of] the loss of consensus in the Jewish community. There are fewer people who buy into central messages."

The one issue that increases group consciousness in the Jewish community is Christianity, which symbolizes an external boundary and creates a strong corporate order. Those individuals who cross or straddle boundaries are particularly dangerous because they threaten the existing classification system in a fundamental way. According to Douglas, they blur the lines between the pure and the impure: "Where the social system requires people to hold dangerously ambiguous roles, these persons are credited with uncontrolled, unconscious, dangerous, disapproved powers" (1970:120). Messianic Jews fall between categories and therefore are more threatening than if they were outside Judaism altogether. Douglas states that there is power in the gray, marginal, and inarticulate area (1966:118) Likewise, there is power in the attempt to join, as Messianic believers have done, that which should be separate. Rabbi Greenbaum made this point succinctly when he said, "I say to Messianic Jews . . . 'If you want to be a Christian, be one. Just don't tell me you're a Jew.'" (see also Mirsky 1978.) Although my respondents preferred not to see Jews "cross over" to Christianity, they agreed that it is far easier to deal with such crossing over than with those apostates who have a foot in each religious system.

The driving force behind this seemingly universal rejection throughout the American Jewish community is the Messianics' very reason for being—their attempt to bridge a centuries-old, profoundly painful gap between Jews and Christians. Messianics symbolize the suffering that Jews have endured for nearly two millennia.

The Jewish community has long been concerned about the apostasy of its young people. North American Jews tolerate great diversity, including religious diversity. If Messianic Jews are thoroughly Jewish in their culture and self-identity, why, then, do Jews—elites and others—condemn Messianics with such fervor?

Jews have been proselytized by Christians since the advent of Christianity, thus their reaction to proselytization incorporates those two thousand years of historical pressure (*Christianity Today* 1988). During all that time, "Jews have been resisting with notable resiliency" (Brickner 1978:10). Conversion, for Jews, connotes "joining the enemy" (Isser and Schwartz 1980:63). Those who assimilated often did so by hiding their Jewishness by changing their name, avoiding Jewish family and friends, and converting to Christianity. They severed their connections to their people and their past, and they gave up an ethnic and religious life (Bershtel and Graubard 1992). For example, Jews who left their communities during the Middle Ages were absorbed, within a few generations, into the general population (Wirth 1956 [1928]).

Missionary activity expressed an ancient hostility that seemingly threatened the existence of the Jewish people. At the very least it called into question the legitimacy of Jewish survival in the modern world (Endelman 1987). Even those who converted often had to contend with the notion of Jewishness as a hereditary trait. In strongly anti-Semitic societies, Jewish character was considered inflexible and thus impervious to baptism (Endelman 1987).

Today the Jewish community still considers Jewish character immutable.[4] This sentiment is expressed in a traditional joke, repeated here in one of its many variations.

> Four Jewish apostates met on a train in Russia and began to relate the reasons that prompted them to accept Christianity. The first apostate said that he had saved himself from a pogrom by changing his religion. "The Cossacks killed almost every Jew in the village," he explained, "so I converted."
>
> The second apostate stated that he had wanted desperately to attend the university, but since Jews were not admitted he had become a Christian so that he might continue his education.
>
> The third apostate explained that he had fallen madly in love with a beautiful Gentile girl and that she would not marry him unless he accepted her faith.
>
> When the fourth apostate related his story he said, "I became a Christian because I was convinced that Christianity is superior to . . ."
>
> "Now wait a minute," interrupted one of the Christian converts. "Tell that to your *Gentile* friends!"
> (Adapted from Spalding 1969.)

Conversion, then, touches on the historic feelings of a community that has been persecuted for centuries and has maintained itself through separation from the rest of society. This attitude is expressed in the following poem:

They are Goyim [Gentiles],
Foes of the faith,
Beings of darkness,
Drunkards and bullies,
Swift with the fist or the bludgeon,
Many in species, but all
Engendered of God for our sins,
and many and strange their idolatries,
But the worst of the Goyim are the
creatures called Christians.
(Zangwill in Wirth 1956 [1928]:119.)

Before 1967, missionary activity in North America did not represent much of a threat to Jews. It was confined to a small fringe element of American Christianity and was a minor item on the visible agenda of mainline Protestant and Catholic bodies. Organizations such as the American Board of Missions to the Jews were also considered fringe groups, and thus were disregarded by both Jewish and mainline Christian organizations.

In June 1967, however, Dr. Carl Henry, editor of *Christianity Today*, called for an ecumenical pooling of resources in order to "spread the Gospel." The first meeting, held in 1969 and attended by Fundamentalists, was organized by Dr. Henry and the Rev. Billy Graham (*American Jewish Committee Memorandum* 1972; *The Star* 1973). Planning continued over the next four years, and in January 1973, more than 140 Christian groups launched the largest evangelical campaign in history. Their approach, which depended on the mass media and on door-to-door canvassing, was to "call the continent to Christ" by confronting everybody in North America with the gospel. They called their movement Key73. According to one Key73 leader, the program could convert the world to Christianity in one or two years. This leader stated that one-fourth of the world's population is Christian. If every Christian converted one person within the year and if all of those persons converted the rest, everyone would be Christian in two years (Bernards 1973).

At this point, Key73 was no longer an exclusively Fundamentalist group, it now comprised mainline Protestant churches, Catholic dioceses, independent Evangelical groups, church bodies, para-ecclesiastical groups and other organizations that had never worked together before (*American Jewish Committee Memorandum* 1972; *New York Times* 1973a; *Texas Methodist* 1972). The structure of Key73 was loose but inclusive. The contribution expected was relative to the size of the group, local endeavors were financed by the local church, and participation was determined by the parish. In short, Key73 had gained mainstream respectability. Cars around the country displayed bumper stickers with slogans such as "I Found It" or "Jesus Saves."[5]

The Jewish community, led by Rabbi Marc H. Tanenbaum, national director of the American Jewish Committee's interreligious affairs department, responded to Key73 with alarm and concern. Not only did Jews have to deal with Key73, but many Jewish youths were joining more marginal new religious movements (NRMs) as well. For many Jews this was a frightening time that sparked visions of the Holocaust; their response was nationwide mobilization.

Death and apostasy have never been differentiated clearly by Jews, as evidenced by the well-known Jewish custom of "sitting *shiva*"—mourning as dead a Jew who converts or even marries outside the religion. This notion has gained wide recognition among non-Jews as well through movies and theater productions such as *Fiddler on the Roof*, in which converted and intermarried youths are mourned by their parents and family and are never mentioned again. The Holocaust reinforced these insular attitudes; death and apostasy, persecution and conversion, all blended into a major threat.

Rabbi Tanenbaum warned that after the Nazis had destroyed one-third of the Jewish population, Soviet assimilation would take another third and conversion would wipe out the remainder (*Texas Methodist* 1972). Jews perceived that thirty years after millions of Jews had been lost to the Nazis, now again (after the vow "never again"), countless Jewish children were being lost to NRMs and missionaries.

Elie Wiesel, a Holocaust survivor, described a Polish-Jewish Holocaust survivor who "lost" a son to a NRM.

> He could not understand what had happened, asking, "Did I
> survive in order to fail precisely where my ancestors
> triumphed? To give life to a renegade?" He sobbed, and I
> was barely able to console him. (1988:161.)

In a similar vein, Marianne Langer Zeitlin (1984:33) wrote that when her son was "taken" from her by the Divine Light Mission, her loss "turned the clock [back] to Holocaust time." Even the 1978 mass suicide at the People's Temple in Jonestown, Guyana conjured up memories of Nazi death camps for many Jews (Hecht 1985; Kollin 1979).[6]

Holocaust imagery also appears frequently in Jewish anticult literature. Some anticultists believe that new religious movements are so authoritarian and so antidemocratic as to endanger the society at large as well as their converts, at both the psychological and the physical level. Indeed, NRMs have been likened to anti-Semitic movements, and the fate of their devotees to the fate of those who were interned in Auschwitz (Rudin and Rudin 1980:29).[7]

Some NRMs encourage this analogy, perhaps unwittingly, by denying that the Holocaust ever occurred. One group, The Way International, has "promoted anti-Semitic propaganda claiming the Holocaust was a 'hoax'" (Schwartz 1982:11). Neri (1984:44) corroborated this point when she noted that The Way describes the Holocaust as "Zionist propaganda." The Unification Church ("Moonies") is also considered anti-Semitic because of its explanation of the Holocaust: The Rev. Moon argues that the six million Jews who died in the Holocaust were paying indemnity for the crucifixion of Jesus. Although these new religious movements have said many things that the Jewish community might consider anti-Semitic, the statements employing Holocaust imagery have provoked the strongest responses.

Rabbi Tanenbaum feared that Jews would be sought after and evangelized by Key73. The Rev. Theodore A. Raedeke, executive director of Key73, assured Tanenbaum that the campaign had no anti-Semitic implications and would not "persecute, pressure or force Jews to believe or do anything against their will" (*New York Times* 1973a; *Texas Methodist* 1973a). Even so, the Jewish community remained fearful, knowing that groups that were seeking to evangelize Jews would attach themselves to the national effort (*Street'n Steeple* 1972). This happened, in fact; Messianic Jews capitalized on Key73, riding on its coattails as people with a special mission to the Jews.

The Rabbinical Council of America, which represents more than a thousand Orthodox rabbis in the United States and Canada, made the following statement in 1973:

The enthusiasm which Key73 will no doubt generate should
alert the Jewish community, and we ask all segments of the
Jewish community to be on the alert lest the over-
zealousness of this effort begin to penetrate into the Jewish
communities. Already we have had reports of such activities
on the college campus and in a number of smaller Jewish
communities. (*New York Times* 1973a.)

Slowly, the churches involved began to issue formal statements that they did
not aim to convert Jews. The Rev. Billy Graham also declared that proselytizing seeks to commit people against their will:

Gimmicks, coercion and intimidation have no place in my
evangelistic efforts . . . I have never felt called to single out
the Jews as Jews nor to single out any particular groups,
cultural, ethnic, or religious. (*Newsweek* 1973; *Texas
Methodist* 1973b.)

Although Graham's statement carried weight among Evangelicals and
therefore was a triumph for the Jewish community, the overriding feeling
among Jews was that all of the Jewish-Christian dialogues in the past had
been in vain, and that future dialogue had possibly been damaged by Key73
(*Maryland Baptist* 1972b; *Methodist Reporter* 1973; *New York Times* 1973d;
Western Recorder 1973a, 1973b). Rabbi Ben-Tzion Kravitz believes that this
sentiment was compounded by the feeling that Key73 had served as "the
launching pad" for Christian groups such as Jews for Jesus that proselytize
specifically among Jews. Indeed, many other evangelizing Christian NRMs
were gaining momentum in the United States at the same time as Key73.

According to some observers, the Jewish response was so strong that it
backfired. Indeed, the Jewish community is credited with giving Key73 the
momentum it needed by becoming more excited about it than did many Christian groups (*New York Baptist* 1973). Before the Jews responded, Key73 was
unable to attract media attention (*United Methodist Reporter* 1973a). Rabbi
Henry Siegman, executive vice-president of the Synagogue Council of

America, noted that many Christians had not heard of Key73, but virtually all
North American Jews knew about it. He was angered by "the imputations of
Jewish insecurity and internal weakness implicit in this defensiveness—as if
Judaism stands on so frail a reed as to be blown away by the slightest wind
that comes along" (*New York Times* 1973b:50). Certainly the Jewish response
was an important element in the longevity of Key73. Dr. Raedeke remarked
that "their [the Jewish] reaction helped our cause" by keeping Key73 in the
headlines (*New York Times* 1973d; see also *New York Baptist* 1973; *Texas
Methodist* 1973c).

The strong Jewish reaction to Key73 may have been largely a matter of
timing. In the 1970s, the Jewish community was fighting simultaneous as-
saults by Christian evangelists and by more marginalized NRMs and perhaps
were on the defensive as a result. At that time, many youths were joining
NRMs, and while the Christian community also felt the threat posed by "cults,"
people from Jewish backgrounds were (and still are) represented dispropor-
tionately among the members of new religious movements.[8]

Although the Key73 tempest ultimately subsided and is now virtually
forgotten, the concerns it raised came at a time when NRMs were gaining
strength, NRMs based in Christianity, such as Messianic Judaism, intensified
the threat. Although the Messianic Jewish movement claims its origins in the
first century C.E., it gained numerical and organizational strength in the early
1970s. Rabbi Greenbaum, a rabbinic student at the time, recalled those days:

> Let's put it [Key73] in context. It was right after the hippie
> days, sort of the tail end of the Jesus freak days, and a little
> bit of Messianic Judaism days, and Christianity had become
> sort of hip for five minutes. And I think it threatened a lot of
> Jews.

Jewish spokespeople today generally believe that acculturation is the
main threat to the American Jewish community. The "melting pot" that is
United States society seems to be more effective than proselytization at encouraging assimilation. By the 1960s, American Jews began to "look" like
other Americans; they were viewed by others and by themselves as belonging to the mainstream, and they began assimilating dominant cultural forms

that no longer seemed foreign (Moore 1994). Historically, Jews had been excluded from the larger society and thus were left with no choice but to maintain ties "among their own." Indeed, leaving Judaism would have meant joining those who attacked friends, family, and community. As long as societies were static and the boundaries between them impermeable, as long as religious hatred and persecution of the Jews continued, the existence of the Jewish people was assured. That existence was not threatened until many barriers to the secular world were removed and the larger society opened to Jews. This removal of barriers has weakened the boundaries of the Jewish community, however. At the beginning of the 1990s, assimilation by intermarriage was the greatest threat, since approximately one-quarter of North American Jews were married to Gentiles (Kosmin et al. 1990; Medding et al. 1992). By comparison, the numerical threat of NRMs is relatively small, but they provide a focus for anxiety about assimilation.

> What the Spanish failed to do in the Inquisition, what Pius
> IX failed to do through his edicts and actions, what the Nazis
> failed to do in the Holocaust, may yet occur through the
> apparent gentleness of the "Krishnas" and the "Moonies,"
> the "Jews for Jesus" and others who speak the language of
> the disenchanted. (Isser and Schwarz 1980:72.)

WHAT THE JEWISH COMMUNITY IS DOING TO SAFEGUARD ITS BOUNDARIES

According to the 1990 census of the Council of Jewish Federations, only 62 percent of the U.S. Jewish population who were born Jews currently identify themselves as Jews. Sixteen percent were born Jews and claim no religious identification; 3 percent have converted out; 16 percent were born of Jewish parents but were raised, or are being raised, in another religion (3 percent are unaccounted for) (Kosmin et al. 1990).

How has the North American Jewish community responded to the changes behind these numbers? What has the Jewish community been doing to combat these perceived threats to its integrity? According to the Simon

Wiesenthal Center's Rabbi Cooper,

> I don't think it's too late for the American Jewish
> community, but I think that if the trends continue . . . we will
> be numerically diminished and spiritually devalued.

Cooper believes that the best way to combat these forces is to get Jews into a
Jewish context.

> We have to give them positive reasons to identify Jewishly.
> If we don't, they will disappear. And what might happen is
> that their only reminders of being Jewish would be an anti-
> Semitic act or attacks against Jews . . . that is not enough of a
> reason to want to be Jewish and stay Jewish.

After all, he says,

> The key to Jewish identity is education and Jewish
> experiences. You can read all the books that you want about
> the Sabbath, but if you've never tasted a good piece of
> homemade *challah* [traditional braided egg bread], it's just
> not gonna work.

Part of the problem of identity, according to Rabbi Greenbaum of the
American Jewish Committee, is that

> Jews don't know what makes them different from anybody
> else. I don't know that we're doomed, but . . . we have to
> straighten up and say "We are essentially no different from
> anyone else, but as Jews, we look at the world somewhat
> differently, and that's fine."

He stresses one important thing for Jews to remember:

> Every Jew today is a Jew by choice, because every Jew can
> walk [leave]. Or every Jew can simply not participate. In the

old days, you had to leave. You don't even have to leave
[today]. You just have to not embrace.

Greenbaum views intermarriage and assimilation as just the "tip of the ice-
berg." On one hand, he points out, we send our children to secular universi-
ties to interact with "other people" and to become as Americanized as possible,
lopping "off the rough edges and speech pattern[s] and becoming less Jewish, becoming civilized." Yet at the same time, he says, we are dismayed at
the growth of assimilation.

One response to the threats to Jewish integrity has been the development of an anticult movement (ACM), and there are now two large Jewish
anticult and antimissionary movements in the United States, one secular and
one religous. The first is conducted by the Jewish Federation Council, which
operates the Commission on Cults and Missionaries as well as a Cult Clinic.
The Commission, a branch of the Jewish Community Relations Council, focuses on educating the community about NRMs. The Cult Clinic, operated
though Jewish Family Services, is a secular and nonsectarian agency offering counseling and referral services to people who have been affected by a
cult. According to Rachel Andres, of Los Angeles's Commission on Cults
and Missionaries, the anticult work done in the Jewish Federation Council's
centers in New York and Los Angeles, is primarily anticult, and is intended to
promote awareness of cults.

The other active Jewish anticult and countermissionary movement, Jews
for Judaism, devotes its energy to countermissionary activities. Founded in
Los Angeles, this organization has six offices in North America, mostly on
the East Coast. As a religious group, Jews for Judaism works independently
of the non-Jewish ACM and focuses on educating Jews and providing religious counseling.[9] Its aim is to bring Jews back to religious Orthodoxy.

The Jewish community gains more comfort from defining who is *not* a
member of the community than from defining who *is*. The proverbial line in
the sand is drawn at Jesus's feet. Atheists and agnostics, the so-called "foxhole
Jews," are welcome. Followers of Jesus, however, by whatever name, are
still Christians. Whether they call themselves Hebrew Christians, Messianic
Jews, or Jews for Jesus, in the eyes of the normative Jewish community they
are Christians all the same, "the worst of the *Goyim*." These self-identified
Jews have become a symbolic threat to the Jewish community. Of all the

proselytizers, Christians who identify as Jews are held in the lowest esteem because of their attempt to merge Judaism with Christianity, an attempt that the collective Jewish psyche, with all its scars and prejudices, finds repugnant.

This exclusionary response of the Jewish community has created problems for the self-definition of Messianic Jews, yet it has simultaneously helped to shape that definition. Despite the overlap of two communities, the Christian and the Jewish, Messianic Believers belong to neither. By crossing institutional boundaries, Messianic Judaism threatens the social structure of the Jewish community; Jews thus believe that Messianic Judaism allows individuals to "have their cake and eat it too" by melding the richness of their Jewish heritage with the dominant culture. Messianic Jews, however, view their Christian identity as an extension of their Jewish identity.

Chapter 3

The History of Messianic Judaism
The Movement and the Congregation

Messianic Believers, who now have about 180 active synagogues worldwide,[1] trace their roots to the Jewish Christians of the first century C.E. The term *Jewish Christians* is an umbrella term that designates Jews who are also Christian. As a very broad term that encompasses Messianic Judaism as well as Hebrew Christianity, it tells us nothing about the level of Jewish ethnic identity or the branch of Christianity embraced by the group or individual.[2] As with Jewish Christian movements of generations past, the central struggle of Messianic Judaism today for self-definition revolves around the degree to which it identifies Jewishly ("Judaizes") at both the congregational and the individual level.

THE BIRTH OF THE MOVEMENT

The first Jewish Christians, in the first century C.E. were Jesus and his disciples, who were born Jewish, observed Judaism, and believed that Jesus was the Messiah. This belief did not remove them or their followers from the Jewish community. By the end of the century, however, an ideological separation between Judaism and Christianity had occurred, and it was no longer possible to be a Jewish Christian and be accepted by either the Jewish or the

43

Christian community; both communities required renouncement of the other (Harris-Shapiro 1992; LaMagdeleine 1977).

Forcible conversion of Jews to Christianity has a long and bloody history, dating back at least as far back as the Holy Land Crusades of the eleventh through thirteenth centuries C.E. In contrast, twentieth-century conversion efforts have been characterized by the use of reason rather than force (Sobel 1974). England is widely believed to be the home of the "intellectual stimulus" behind this shift. The first Jewish Christian society, the London Society for Promoting Christianity Amongst the Jews, was formed in 1809. Dozens of similar groups formed elsewhere in early nineteenth-century England. All of them worked in a Christian context and viewed their converts as Christians who came from Hebrew (Jewish) backgrounds but who ceased to be culturally Jewish after their conversion. Some of the societies evangelized actively, regarding themselves as Jews bearing a Jewish message to fellow Jews; others simply offered financial aid. Most of these societies, however, were short-lived (LaMagdeleine 1977; Sobel 1974).

The American movement followed in the steps of the British movement. In the United States, missionary activity burgeoned in the second half of the nineteenth century (Sobel 1974), but associations did not begin to form until the very end of that century. For example, the American Board of Missions to the Jews (ABMJ) was founded by Leopold Cohn, a Hungarian Jew who immigrated to the United States in 1892, under dubious circumstances (Eichhorn 1978). Cohn opened a mission in Brooklyn that was supported by the American Baptist Home Missionary Society. In 1894 he founded another mission, the Williamsburg Mission to the Jews, Inc., which changed its name in 1924 to the American Board of Missions to the Jews.[3] The change of name symbolized a vision of an outreach that went beyond the northeast to encompass the entire country (LaMagdeleine 1977).

The American Board of Missions to the Jews retained its name and founding ideology until the mid-1980s (Kohn 1985). Although it maintains its official name, the group also calls itself The Chosen People. This new name suggests an increased emphasis on Jewish identity, as does the fact that the group now encourages members to attend weekly services at ABMJ synagogues rather than at Christian churches. Now that The Chosen People is well established, it does not need to emphasize similarity to Gentiles, but can emphasize Jewish tradition to better serve the needs of the Jewish Christian community.

Most of the Jewish Christian organizations established in the nineteenth century are no longer active. Fewer than twenty reached their fiftieth birthday, and only a handful survive today. Among them are:

- Church's Ministry Amongst the Jews, which used to be the London Society for Promoting Christianity amongst Jews and was founded in 1809.
- International Society for the Evangelization of the Jews, which was founded in 1842 as the British Society for the Propagation of the Gospel among the Jews.
- British Messianic Jewish Alliance (BMJA), which was born in Britain as the Hebrew Christian Alliance in 1866.
- Messianic Testimony, a relatively new British missionary entity that was born in 1973 from the combination of two much older groups, the Mildmay Mission to the Jews (established in 1876) and the Testimony to Israel (established in 1893).
- American Messianic Fellowship, which was established in 1887 as the Chicago Hebrew Mission.
- American Board of Missions to the Jews.

As indicated by the large number of name changes and mergers, the societies that survived were adept at keeping pace with the rapidly progressing "Judaization" of Jewish Christianity, a term I use to mean the increase in Jewish cultural tradition, independent of religiosity.[4] This trend toward Judaization is also evident in the International Messianic Jewish (Hebrew Christian) Alliance, which was founded as the International Hebrew Christian Alliance in 1925. The International Alliance was formed as an umbrella organization to unite alliances around the world. According to a 1994 issue of the organization's journal, *The Messianic Jew (and Hebrew Christian)*, the Alliance includes groups in the United States (Messianic Jewish Alliance of America, MJAA), Great Britain (BMJA), Canada, Israel, Argentina, Australia, Brazil, France, Germany, the Netherlands, New Zealand, South Africa, Switzerland, and Uruguay.

The majority of the large organizations today are no longer backed by Christian groups, but operate independently, and their leaders are often open in their Jewish identification, proudly displaying their Hebrew names and prayer accessories. Messianic Judaism leads this trend toward increased Judaization.

Today there are two Messianic "denominations" in the United States, the Union of Messianic Jewish Congregations and the Messianic Jewish Alliance of America. The MJAA (previously known as the Hebrew Christian Alliance of America, HCAA) was formed in 1915 by Hebrew Christians in "good standing in the Evangelical churches in America" after a series of conferences that began in 1901 (Sobel 1974). The main purpose of this group was to evangelize Jews and to provide a support structure for Hebrew Christians. It did not originally support a strong Jewish identity after conversion; rather, it encouraged the converted Jews to become more Gentile-like in order to be "honorable." The HCAA viewed Jewish practices and customs as no more than an aid to conversion and a helpful mechanism for Jews in the transition to Christianity (LaMagdeleine 1977).

When the HCAA changed its name to the Messianic Jewish Alliance of America in 1975, the impetus came from younger members; the new name reflected the changing dynamics within the group. Members believed that Messianic Jewish Alliance of America described their beliefs more accurately than the old name, and by changing *Christian* to *Messianic* and replacing *Hebrew* with *Jewish*, they adopted less offensive equivalents. This terminology reflected the new members' concern with maintaining their Judaism while accepting Jesus as Messiah (Rausch 1982a). Today the MJAA remains a principal support structure and information network for Messianic Jews.

The Union of Messianic Jewish Congregations began much later, initially as a source of support for congregations rather than individuals. It was founded in 1979 with nineteen charter congregations and grew to twenty-five within the first few years. The purpose was to "facilitate a national intercongregation development" of Messianic Judaism (Rausch 1982a:191). Although the UMJC started with the intention of complementing the role of the MJAA, the two have developed into competing "denominations."[5] Adat haRuach belongs to the latter, which operates its own *yeshiva* (seminary), primarily through correspondence courses, and provides educational material for children.

When Messianic Judaism emerged as a viable form of worship in the late 1960s, it paralleled the growth of the Jesus movement (Quebedeaux 1978), but it did not officially coalesce until Messiah '75, a national conference that drew six hundred Messianic Jews from all over the world (Liberman 1976). Messianic Judaism has grown from a handful of members in 1975 to a substantial movement today, although it is very difficult to obtain accurate numbers of Messianic Believers. An educated estimate, based on Schiffman's numbers (1992) is between fifteen and twenty thousand. This is consistent with other observations, which estimate the number of Messianic Jews to be approximately ten thousand (Isaacs 1997 [personal communication]; Bernstein 1997).[6]

The appeal and growth of Messianic Judaism can be explained in part by Roof's observations (1993) on the growth of conservative religious trends and NRMs among baby boomers, and in part by the growth of ethnicity and ethnic pride over the past thirty years. Many scholars believe that Jews began to identify more strongly with their heritage after the State of Israel was established in 1948. Some attribute the rapid growth of Messianic Judaism to the Arab-Israeli Six-Day War of 1967 and think the war marks the beginning of a greater Jewish consciousness among Jews (Liberman 1976; Rausch 1982a). Danzger (1989) points out that the 1967 war was a turning point for Jews throughout the Diaspora, he suggests it provided an impetus to explore Jewish identity. According to Glazer (1972), the war was the largest, but not the only, event that led North American Jews to feel it was necessary to reinforce boundaries that were being eroded in the United States.[7]

These explanations of the growth of the Messianic movement, however, fall short in that they address only the timing, not the direction, of the shift: The historical backdrop of the 1960s may explain an increase in Jewish consciousness, but it does not account for the growth of Jewish Christianity, specifically Messianic Judaism. Among Hebrew Christians, it is understandable that an increase in pride and awareness of their heritage moved them toward a more Judaizing expression of their Christianity, but still, it does not follow that there should be a movement of mainstream Jews to a Christian belief system. Nor does it follow that these events would increase the appeal of Messianic Judaism for Gentiles, who are estimated to make up about half of all Messianic Believers nationwide.

I believe that the numbers of Messianic Believers are increased in two ways. Jews are recruited via the Messianic "Judaization" of traditional proselytizing rhetoric, which makes a Christian message more palatable to them. Gentiles, on the other hand, are attracted by the opportunity to adopt a new ethnic and a new religious identity simultaneously, thereby achieving a special ethnic status that otherwise would have eluded them. In their search for a closer, more authentic relationship with Jesus, the opportunity to worship in the style of the first century church appeals to them.

Messianic Jews understand clearly how problematic Christian imagery is for many Jews; and recognizing that Christian symbols are synonymous with persecution in the collective Jewish psyche, Messianic Jews attempt to remove this obstacle. For example, the hellenized name *Jesus* creates problems for Jews; therefore Messianic Jews call Jesus by his Hebrew name, Yshua. Likewise, *convert, Christ, Christian, New Testament*, and *cross* have euphemisms of their own: *Convert* becomes *completed* or *fulfilled Jew*; Christ is called Yshua or Mashiach (Hebrew for Messiah); *Christian* becomes *Believer; New Testament* becomes *New Covenant;* and *cross* becomes *tree* (Liberman 1976). The belief within Messianic Judaism is that it is up to Jewish Believers to "witness to Jews" (Juster and Pawley 1981; *Messianic Times* 1992a). As the author of an editorial in *The Messianic Times* (1992a), the Toronto based international newsletter, pointed out, no group is more aware of the hostility to the gospel than Jewish Believers. As one Adat haRuach ethnic Jew lamented, "that antagonism is the cultural gap that separates us from our people. We understand the emotional power that Yshua himself must have felt as he looked down on Jerusalem and wept."

For this reason many Messianics cringe when they are mistaken for members of Jews for Jesus. Messianic Jews go out of their way to make their message palatable to mainstream Jewry, donning their *tallit* (prayer shawl) and *kippot* and reciting Hebrew prayers on the Jewish Sabbath. Jews for Jesus, on the other hand, worship on Sundays in churches with pews and choirs and organs and crosses. When I first heard of Messianic Judaism, I (like many others) did not know that there were groups of Jews who believed in Jesus but were not affiliated with those young men and women in jeans jackets who handed out offensively humorous tracts at my undergraduate institution.

Torn between the belief that Messianic Believers must "spread the word" and their awareness that aggressive proselytizing is often offensive to American Jews, Messianic Jews work to find a balance. One fundamental way they do this is by presuming that the majority of Jews "become completed" not through public evangelistic activity but through congregational friendships and family (see also Neitz 1987). Therefore they encourage personal relationships over more traditional proselytizing techniques (*The Messianic Times* 1992a).

Part of the appeal Messianic Judaism holds for recruits is the ethnic "status" that Jewish identification confers. Being ethnic makes people feel unique and special while giving them a sense of belonging to a collectivity. The symbolic ethnicity of Messianic Judaism gives individuals the appearance of conformity, but with the element of choice (see Waters 1990). Every recruit I interviewed placed a high value on the ability to "be Jewish"[8] and still worship Yshua. They have found a way to distinguish themselves ethnically, through Judaism, without giving up their connection to the religious element of choice, Christianity.

THE BIRTH OF A CONGREGATION

Adat haRuach is one of about 300 Messianic congregations in North America (Isaacs 1997).[9] The largest of the three Messianic congregations in El Leon, a large city in Southern California, it is also one of the larger congregations in the United States. Messianic services in this country are attended by twenty-six to one hundred persons, on average (Harris-Shapiro 1992; Schiffman 1992), whereas on a given Saturday, from 150 to two hundred persons worship at Adat haRuach.[10] The majority of Messianic services, including those of Adat haRuach, are held in borrowed or rented spaces (see Schiffman 1992; Stokes 1994; see also Miller 1997; Warner and Wittner 1998).

Adat haRuach has grown steadily since it was founded in 1981 by fifteen members, and fairly rapidly in comparison with many synagogues. However, Rabbi Jason points out that the congregation is not growing at the same rate as some Evangelical churches (he cites the Calvary Chapels, where membership often reaches a thousand in the first six months) because the

Messianic movement has a smaller clientele; it draws from Messianic Jews and Gentiles who have a Jewish vision.

Many nonmembers attend this congregation regularly and participate in the weekly activities. To become a member, one is required to attend membership classes or, if none are then being offered, to listen to a series of tapes about the purpose of the congregation and the responsibilities of its members. One must profess agreement with Adat haRuach's doctrinal statement and also submit a written copy of one's testimony. Testimonies are personal accounts of salvation, healing, and/or miracles and are usually shared within the context of a religious service. In the case of applicants for membership, however, they are written accounts that have an emphasis on when and how the individual came to the Lord.

The congregation is supported not by membership fees but by donations. Tithing is important and is done privately. All congregants can participate in congregational activities, and Adat haRuach sponsors a range of group meetings. Congregants are welcome and encouraged to attend these meetings, although only members can lead the various ministries and be in positions of representation. For example, only members can vote on congregational issues and be elected to positions such as Elder. Also, only members can join the dance troupe that visits other churches, but anyone can dance along with the Dance Ministry at less formal occasions, including Adat haRuach worship services.

The groups at Adat haRuach include the Women's Ministry, Men's Ministry, Single's Ministry, Dance Ministry, Music Ministry, havorah (among Messianic believers the equivalent to home fellowship), Bible Study, and a group for teens. These ministries develop out of, and are intended to be a response to, the variety of spiritual and social needs the congregation exhibits (see also Miller 1997).

Adat haRuach's membership consists of about 60 percent ethnic Jews and 40 percent Gentiles, a mix that Rabbi Jason thinks is typical of Messianic congregations. (His count favors Jews, but my count found a more equal distribution.)[11] This ratio dissatisfies some ethnic Jews, who would prefer a larger Jewish membership. Some members regard Adat haRuach as ten years behind the rest of the Messianic movement in terms of its Messianic vision. Tammy, a Messianic Jew who has been involved in the movement for over a decade, believes that a larger Jewish membership would increase the congregation's Jewishness. Sometimes she hears people refer to Adat haRuach as "church" and to Yshua as "Jesus"; she is annoyed and frustrated by this, and views it as evidence that the Messianic vision at Adat haRuach is lacking.

Adat haRuach tries to bridge the gap between Jews and Gentiles by emphasizing what Messianic Believers have in common. Because the range of congregants' religious backgrounds is quite varied, the common denominator is maintained, and many theological issues take a backseat to maintaining an emphasis on the Jewishness of the faith. For example, opinions about the devil or about heaven and hell vary from individual to individual, and no attempt is ever made to address them. Likewise, expression of the gifts of the spirit is something that many congregants experience, but they are encouraged to do so in private. In part, this is because of the concern that Jews may be put off—either through fright or judgment of craziness. When the gifts of the spirit are exhibited, usually in the form of speaking in tongues or of healing, it is done in a quiet corner somewhere or in the individuals' homes. Occasionally, newcomers to Adat haRuach will receive a gift of the spirit, but these situations are ended quickly.

Adat haRuach also tries to bridge the gap between ethnicities, ages, and marital statuses. Of the seventy-seven families in the congregation's roster (which includes members' photos, addresses, and phone numbers), nineteen are either Latino, African American, or Asian American. All ages are represented in the congregation, from small children to seniors, but the majority are baby boomers and their families. All but two of the thirty people I formally interviewed were in their thirties or forties. Men and women are represented equally among the single members, except for single parents, a rather large category. Twelve of the seventy-seven households are single-parent families; ten of these parents are women.

Half of my respondents had bachelor's degrees, and two had vocational degrees. Three had graduate degrees—one was the Messianic rabbi, who had attended seminary; and the others were Ph.D.'s. This number does not represent the educational background of most Adat haRuach congregants, however; in my time there, I met only two other individuals with advanced degrees, a psychologist and a lawyer.

All but six of my interviewees were already "saved" when they came to Messianic Judaism.[12] Those who came from other religious groups were primarily from neocharismatic/Pentecostal churches such as the Vineyard Christian Fellowship, Calvary Chapel, the International Church of the Four-square Gospel, or nondenominational churches. Those of Jewish background spoke of their first time at Adat haRuach as a "coming home" experience and described a sense of "relief" (see also Eiesland 1997). One respondent felt that he was "returning to what I've gone astray [from], what I've left . . . returning to [my] roots." Indeed, many of the Jews realized that they had Jewish backgrounds, or became identified with Judaism, only after they began attending services at a Messianic congregation. The Messianic Gentiles, on the other hand, said that they were attracted to the movement because of the authenticity of the worship.

The Messianic movement is so small (or Adat haRuach is so active) that in *The Messianic Times* I read about people I had met or heard about through other members. In the winter of 1992, for example, the newspaper ran a story titled, "Messianic Believers in Jerusalem Open up Crisis Pregnancy Center," about Israel's first pro-life association. This center was started by a couple who formerly had attended Adat haRuach, and its Messianic activities are supported financially by the congregation. (Adat haRuach also supports a family in Russia and a congregation in South America.)

In an attempt to be heard by Jews, Adat haRuach recruits adherents through activities that members do not categorize as aggressive and are unlike those of their Jews for Jesus counterparts, whose proselytizing strategies include knocking on front doors, street evangelism, developing cell groups, conducting educational seminars, hospitality outreaches, and selling books door-to-door. The congregation uses four major recruiting methods. First, on Sundays, members set up a table in a large park in El Leon. The table is always staffed by the same two men and by anyone else who wants to join them for any part of the day. They cover the table with literature and drape a large banner across the front that identifies them as Messianic Believers. On alternate Sundays, the Dance Ministry joins the group and dances.

Although members encourage people to come to the table, they follow no one, accost no one, and do not shove leaflets into people's hands. On one such Sunday I was told,

> Jews don't want to convert to Christianity. [But] if someone
> comes up and says "Messiah" it's like, "Oh, Messiah, that's
> not a foreign religion." Greek terminology does not
> communicate what we're trying to say.

Messianic Believers point out that while the choice of whether to accept Yshua
is a personal matter, Jews first need to be able to hear the message; and they
cannot hear it if it is couched in traditional Christian language.

As a second method of recruiting, Adat haRuach engages in interfaith
activities such as having members of the congregation make appearances in
Gentile churches. In this form of outreach Rabbi Jason delivers sermons,
hosts Seders, and sometimes even takes over the worship service with the
Music Ministry and the Dance Ministry in tow. The Dance Ministry coordi-
nator says,

> We have that dual vision of not only providing ways for the
> Jewish people to find their Messiah, but also to get out to the
> Gentile churches and show them the Jewishness of their
> faith; we help fight anti-Semitism in that way and promote
> unity.

The busiest time for this type of outreach is Passover, which has long
been a favorite season for interfaith activities because the holiday touches on
common Jewish and Christian themes. Both Gentiles and members' relatives
are invited to Adat haRuach's Seder. Most of the relatives who attend are
Gentiles—either nominal Christians or born-again Christians. Occasionally,
a Jewish Believer's non-Believing family joins in as well. Passover bridges
the two cultures for friends and family.

A third method of outreach is the sponsoring of Messianic events for
the public. One such event was a concert in which Adat haRuach brought in
Alyosha, a Russian Messianic Jew, to perform on the piano. The music
provided a community experience for Messianics that incorporated non-
Believing Jews as well. The turnout was smaller than anticipated because of
heavy rains, but even so, a significant number of Russian non-Believing Jews
attended. At the concert, Rabbi Jason announced that he was hosting a brunch
for the Russians the next morning, giving them a chance to speak with Alyosha

in their native tongue.

The weekly services themselves serve as the fourth type of outreach. As soon as one enters, one is showered with attention. On my first morning at Adat haRuach, I was greeted and welcomed by a woman who gave me a hug and a *Siddur* (prayer book).[13] An elderly gentleman welcomed me and handed me the morning's program. When I could not find a place to sit, someone else ushered me to a seat. To my dismay, we were then asked to break up into groups of four and pray together. After much shuffling of chairs, the couple in front of me asked me to join them, and I had nowhere to run: This type of outreach is taken seriously by regular Adat haRuach attendees. The couple with whom I prayed took me under their wing, introduced me to other people, and made me feel generally comfortable at Adat haRuach in the beginning stages.

Also on that first day, when we were asked to introduce ourselves to someone we didn't know, people who had noticed me as a new face came up from many aisles away, chatted with me, and introduced me to their spouses. When I went up to greet the rabbi after services, someone let me go ahead of him in line, nodding to the rabbi and saying, "A new face." This welcoming attention to new people was unlike anything I had experienced in my Reform congregation while growing up, and (I suspect) was unlike the Adat haRuach members' childhood experiences.

Methods of outreach vary with individuals, but most congregants are wary, if not apologetic, about "in your face" proselytizing. Simon, a Messianic Jew in his early thirties, knows that friends and family members will not develop a relationship with Yshua as a result of his "whipping the Bible out and smacking them with it. It's going to be primarily God's spirit moving their lives." Others in the congregation live by this approach as well, ever cautious about stepping over the line into the realm of "aggressive proselytization." At a Purim party following the Purim service, Peter, another congregant, approached me to ask whether I had enjoyed a musical evening at a nearby Evangelical church. The performer had been Marty Goetz, a nationally popular Messianic Jewish singer and many Adat haRuach congregants had attended. Peter apologized to me, saying he hoped I was not offended by the call to the altar of people who had accepted Yshua into their hearts as a result of the concert. He felt that this was an expression of the church's general insensitivity to Jews. After all, he explained, "That kind of public thing does not appeal to Jews." A lot of people, Peter believes, need to learn that fact and keep it in mind when reaching out to Jews.

My entry into the Messianic community was easy because Believers welcome new people with outstretched arms and, in their desire to live and teach by example, include them in their daily lives. The Adat haRuach community accepted me with apparent ease, largely because I was viewed as being there "for a reason," namely because it was God's plan that I be there. Although they knew that I was there as a sociologist with a research agenda, time and time again they told me that I clearly had a heart for Messianic Judaism. They believed that my acceptance of them (they are used to rejection by the Jewish community) was an indication that I was on a spiritual path and they were happy to know that God had opened this door, this opportunity, regardless of my agenda (see also Gordon 1987; Warner 1988). As I spent more time in the community, congregants occasionally asked me where I was in my belief, or whether I was still "secure" in my beliefs.

If nothing else, my first name marked me as a Jew. And, as a Jew among Messianic Jews, I was a particularly desirable target of their attentions. Certainly they are wary of people coming in on the pretext of social science research, but I found that these reservations existed only among the leaders, not the average adherents. My Jewishness eased acceptance at Adat haRuach in a few ways. It made me an "expert" in Judaism (much to my amusement, given my secular background), and people asked me about the meaning of various things, from holidays to Yiddish expressions. It also made me one of God's chosen people.[14]

Although my entry into the community was smooth, I learned very late in my time at Adat haRuach that my acceptance was not as easy I had thought. One of my interviewees was kind enough to take me into her confidence and explain that I was "a mystery to many." She was unwilling to discuss this on tape, but at another point in the interview she said,

> I don't have any friends that are non-Believers. It's hard to
> carry on a friendship with someone who doesn't share the
> same ideals and beliefs. It's really hard. That's why you're
> such an enigma to so many people—because they feel such

an attachment to you, but yet they don't know how to relate
to you.

This enigma created tension among some of the congregants, primarily the
singles in my general age group, because they had different ideas about how
to relate to me. The respondent who spoke to me believed that I should not be
protected from anything, and therefore that I should be proselytized; anything less would be hypocritical. Others, she explained, were concerned that
if they openly proselytized I would never become a Believer; they felt that
the best way to treat me was with "kid gloves." I was pained to know that I
was causing dissent among some of the congregants and that I had been left
out of so much discussion. At the same time, I was warmed by knowing that
they showed concern over how best to "convert" me. Furthermore, I suddenly understood why, when everybody was praying for Jewish friends to
accept the Lord, nobody ever mentioned me. An example of such kid-glove
treatment can be found in this excerpt from my fieldnotes:

> Late one night, at my car after a funeral, Laura told me that
> she respected my beliefs in the same way that I did hers.
> Confused, I asked her how that could be if she (surely)
> believes I will spend the afterlife in Hell. Her response was
> that that had nothing to do with her respect for me, although
> it did make her sad "that we can't be with you in the next
> life, because I'd like that."

I was concerned that I had apparently constructed a fence around myself that perhaps intimidated congregants or inhibited them from behaving
"naturally" toward me. (This is a salient example of how knowledge in the
field is created by and is a reflection of the interactions between researcher
and respondents.) On further thought, I realized that I had set up the fieldwork so as to evoke this response. I also realized that if I had not done so, I
would not have lasted in the community because of personal discomfort with
overt proselytization. I also know that by reacting as I did, I was able to see
another way in which the congregants respond to people—out-and-out
proselytization may be their preferred method, but it is not their only way. I

was also impressed that they had detected, through subtle cues on my part, my dislike of open proselytization.

Adat haRuach chooses to proselytize in a manner determined largely by the congregants' leader. The son of a Jewish-Gentile marriage, Rabbi Jason was raised neither Christian nor Jewish, although he believes that he and his siblings benefited from both traditions; he grew up without a structured religion, but family events and celebrations acknowledged both backgrounds. In his own words, Jason's knowledge of Judaism "began and ended with a kind of matzo ball soup familiarity." Born and raised on the southern California coast, Jason describes himself as a surfer steeped in the surf culture. After graduating from high school in 1971, he and a friend went to Hawaii to enjoy the waves. While there, he met a group of Christians, began reading the New Testament, and became a Believer. Only later did he identify strongly with Judaism. Today, when he meets people he knew from his surfing days, they are surprised to learn that he is a rabbi; they had not known he was Jewish.

As a Messianic rabbi, Jason is educated in both Christianity and Judaism. After returning from Hawaii, he attended a Christian college and went on to earn a master's degree from an Evangelical Christian seminary. He then spent one year at a Conservative Jewish institution, studying with rabbinic students. Jason states that he did not complete the program because the school would not have ordained him. After satisfying certain requirements, consisting primarily of correspondence courses, he was ordained by the Union of Messianic Jewish Congregation in 1982.

Later, Jason and his wife provided the impetus for establishing Adat haRuach. In 1981 they encouraged a local ministry to help them found a congregation in El Leon, which even though it was a large urban area, had no Messianic congregation at the time. Seventeen years later, he heads one of the largest Messianic synagogues in the country.

The growth of this congregation is particularly interesting in light of the struggle mainline synagogues throughout the country face just to maintain their congregants. Nearly every congregant mentioned that Adat haRuach's growth and stability are due to its close sense of community. I saw this sense of community at work when one congregant, a U.S. Marine, was transferred overseas. On three different occasions, in three different contexts (Bible study, singles, and services), a card or letter addressed to him was passed around for signatures and greetings. One of the cards showed a scene of Jerusalem with a Biblical verse. Beneath all the good wishes was inscribed "We love you and we are praying for God's blessing in Somalia! In Yshua, Your Adat haRuach Family."

In another situation, when a congregant was incarcerated for a crime committed before he became a Believer, the congregation sent him many letters and cards, both collectively and individually. Even though he was imprisoned hundreds of miles away, congregants visited him more than once.

For some, the Adat haRuach family is the closest family they have ever had. As Adam said,

> The thing I like best, I guess, is the sense of family or closeness . . . we're small enough that we actually are a very close family. And that's something I've never felt anywhere else before. . . . it's something I need in my life, to be connected with people. . . . I've always been a loner, so it's a very different place to be.

Missy says that she's found in Adat haRuach what God had always wanted for her, a "true family." She comments, "I've always wanted to be cared for, loved, or [to] fit in, or whatever the case may be."[15]

A tangible measure of this sense of family is the amount of time congregants spend with one another. Most of the time that Wiley spends in activities related to Adat haRuach is social. Simon gave this telling—if slightly convoluted—description of an average week.

> The [Friday night] service, which starts at 8:30 for me because of the men's discipleship, so from 8:30 'till whenever we get out of there, and of course the Bible study, that's every other . . . Thursday. So that's either two or three times a month. . . . And then the play things . . . Saturday night we get together, so that would be say 2 to 10. . . . And Sunday, you know, it's a tough question, because it could be two hours . . . or a full day, or half a day . . .

The Reuttegers note that "there are just so many things going on . . . and we were going to things . . . four or five nights a week." Perhaps Celia and Izzy Eisenstadt put it most succinctly, saying, "Our ministry is our life and our life is the congregation."

Some congregants praised the accountability that such sociability offers. Jessica likes the fact that if she misses a service or is "bummed," congregants notice and "call me and say 'What's wrong? Are you OK? We love you.'" Harry explained that just after they began attending Adat haRuach, his wife, Lacey, went on a business trip.

> I didn't think people even knew me that well. . . . [But] if
> you're not there...people will know, and they wonder, Are
> you sick? And I love that accountability. It helps keep you on
> the track. . . . People from the congregation that I trust are
> there to take care of me.

Another member reports an incident suggesting that such intense sociability exerts powerful social control:

> I remember this one incident where this couple were having
> marital problems, and he thought that he could just more or
> less hide and nobody would know, and he could have his
> little marital problems in private. But with the congregation
> caring about everybody, they noticed right away something
> was wrong, and some of the men went to him while he was
> trying to sort of hide. . . . And so within a very short time
> they worked through the problem rather than him . . . trying
> to ignore it and hide.

Is it possible to maintain this level of intense involvement and emotional investment indefinitely? I found hints to the contrary. On one occasion, for instance, as I listened to the membership tapes from a few years earlier, I did not recognize any of the members' names. When I asked Rabbi Jason about this, he acknowledged that turnover was high at the synagogue, but dismissed it as reflecting a highly transient population and cited the large number of military families.[16]

Consider Lacey, whose husband described the positive aspects of the congregation's intense sociability. She later lamented, "Adat haRuach is like a family, which . . . has its disadvantages in that everybody's got their nose in everybody else's business." Another couple conceded that they finally had to learn how to say "no."

Chapter 4

"Meshuganeh for the Lord"
The Congregants of Adat haRuach

For those following the evolution of the Jewish Christian movement, the last few decades have been particularly interesting. This is in part because of significant growth in the Messianic movement, but also because the movement has shifted from a primarily Christian-centered system of belief to one that increasingly celebrates its Jewish roots. Present-day imagery likens Messianic Judaism to an olive tree that, according to Romans 11:17–22, has been grafted to ensure its strength. The graft represents the Gentiles, and the original tree represents the Messianic Jews. Messianic Judaism does not sanction the conversation of Gentiles to Judaism, but rather teaches that Jews stay Jewish and Gentiles stay Gentiles because the olive tree needs both to maintain its fruitfulness and strength.[1] However, when this teaching is put into practice, it loses its purist ideology. Messianic Believers themselves create a hierarchy in which Messianic Jews are higher than Messianic Gentiles, and this often results in a search for Jewish roots on the part of many Messianic Gentiles.

Messianic Judaism is distinguished from other religious movements by its ability to provide adherents with a new conservative religious expression combined with a new ethnic identity. To illustrate this special feature of Messianic Judaism, I describe members of Adat haRuach who represent the three distinct and characteristic backgrounds: ethnic Jews, Gentiles, and those who reclaim Jewish roots as adults and whom I call "Root Seekers."

SARA, AN ETHNIC JEW

Sara is in her early forties, married to Gabe, with three children. She is very involved in Adat haRuach and is well integrated there. She is of medium build, with short curly dark brown hair. She has an air about her that makes one want to get to know her, and she draws people to her. She and her husband are always flitting about the congregation arranging things, chatting with friends, and managing situations.

Sara was born on Long Island, New York, into a Jewish family. Jewish identification in her childhood home was strong, but her family was not particularly observant; they did not keep kosher or attend synagogue on a weekly basis. She recalls that her grandparents were religious and that visiting them meant keeping plates separate—remembering which were used for dairy and which for meat when setting the table. Sara was sent to her grandparents for High Holidays and other important events, and she remembers fondly those family celebrations. Her parents belonged to a Conservative synagogue, and she herself was *bat mitzvah*; she uses this as a marker of her Jewish upbringing. She also talks about how she didn't really understand the importance of it at the time.

As she was growing up, God was never mentioned in the home or brought up as a topic of discussion, not because the topic was forbidden but because it was never thought about. Sara is quite certain that her parents did not, and do not, believe in God and that there was no spirituality involved in the Jewish traditions that were observed. She grew up viewing the Bible and its stories as a kind of fairy tale. In her own life Sara says that her spirituality "didn't go past tea boxes"—a reference to Celestial Seasons herbal teas with spiritual sayings on the packages.

The cultural aspect of Judaism was very important in Sara's family life, however. For her parents, Judaism meant a set of cultural attributes,

> [It] meant that you were better than everyone else that
> wasn't Jewish, we were special somehow . . . a little

smarter . . . a little, just everything . . . making a certain
amount of money . . . and looking a certain way.

Her parents divided the world into Gentiles and Jews, and they expected their
children to stay within the Jewish world, to not befriend, date, or marry non-
Jews. But Sara was a rebellious girl; she had non-Jewish friends, and she
dated non-Jews, and she eventually married a non-Jew.

In the mid-seventies, when Sara turned twenty, she met Gabe. Gabe's
brother was a born-again Christian who used to talk to Sara about Jesus. She
felt very comfortable around Gabe's brother. She felt that he was a different
kind of man—thoughtful, fun, non-judgmental, and caring—although she
didn't buy his message. For the next ten years, she ran into Christians who
tried to share their message, but Sara felt that their message was for "weak-
lings" for those who couldn't take control of their own lives.

After marrying Gabe, Sara felt isolated. She missed her Jewish background but was ambivalent about becoming "more Jewish" or attending synagogue. She sent her eldest daughter to an Orthodox Jewish preschool in order
to capture some of the "family feeling," but it wasn't until (and as a result of)
the birth of her second child, a son, that she began to think about the world in
spiritual terms. Looking back now, she sees this time as God trying to "open"
her eyes. She began to let her brother-in-law talk to her kids about religion, a
previously forbidden subject. Sara feels it is important for her to stress that
this was a good time in their lives; she and Gabe were happily married and
had just had a healthy and beautiful little boy. They were not, like so many
other Adat haRuach congregants, at "rock bottom" looking to come out of
their darkness. And yet, she remembers, one day she locked herself in the
bathroom and tried to pray. Incredibly, she says, two days later, Rabbi
Jason—at the request of Gabe's brother, who wanted to introduce her to Christianity and felt that the synthesis represented by Messianic Judaism would be
a good first step—called to invite them to services. They went to services and
became Believers the same night.[2] Although the story sounds momentous, as
if she went from "nothing to the truth" literally overnight, Sara stresses that
this is not what happened. From her perspective, God had been guiding her
during the previous ten years. She had begun to change and to understand the
world differently, so her coming to the Lord was a point in the process, not

something that occurred in a vacuum. After she became a Believer, the process continued as her life continued to metamorphose.

Sara's parents were not happy with her religious choices but they had been unhappy with her for other reasons—like for marrying a non-Jew without a secure financial future—previous to her becoming a Believer. Family relations, while strained, continued due to the mutual love that Sara and her mom felt for one another. Sara's brother became a Believer shortly after she did. Her parents find relations with him more divisive because he has not held on to any of his Jewish identity (he is active in a Gentile church) and therefore he seems further out of their reach, with little common ground between them.

After the excitement of that first critical night at Adat haRuach died down, Sara started to pull away and moved toward Gentile churches. It was Gabe who was convinced that Messianic Judaism was where they belonged, and held onto that belief and tried to get his wife to do the same. As Sara started exploring her spirituality and her relationship with God, she became frustrated with the insistence that one could both be Jewish and believe in Jesus. Her focus was on her walk with the Lord, with her spirituality, and not with her ethnicity. After years of continuing to worship at Adat haRuach, Sara feels that she is now able to appreciate her Jewish identity and how it weaves into her faith.

Active members of Adat haRuach, Sara and her husband run a *havorah* (fellowship) on a weekly basis from their home. They socialize frequently and exclusively with Adat haRuach congregants, and Sara was an active mobilizer of the Woman's Ministry (see chapter 7). She is also active in her children's cultural and spiritual growth. Their three children, a teenage daughter and two sons in junior high school, all go to Christian schools. Sara does not work outside the home but rather focuses all her time and energy into the family. She fosters the children's friendships with other Adat haRuach children and spends time organizing activities and driving them to and from other congregants' homes. In the summers her eldest attends Camp Shoshanah, a Messianic Camp in the Adirondack Mountains run by Ariel Ministries of Tustin, California.

Sara is typical of the ethnic Jews I met during my time at Adat haRuach. All of my Jewish informants reported that becoming Messianic had strengthened their Jewish identity and enabled them to transcend the merely cultural aspects of their Jewish upbringing. By establishing what they consider to be a personal relationship with God, these Messianic Believers feel that they have moved beyond the "greeting card" version of Judaism; to have been chosen by God to be Jewish and to have this special relationship with him is a double blessing. For all the ethnic Jews, becoming a Believer and developing a stronger relationship with God has made them more Jewish than ever before. Most Messianic Jews talked about their involvement in a Messianic congregation as a "coming home" experience.

Sara's story also demonstrates another theme common to Messianics at Adat haRuach who are ethnic Jews. All were minimally practicing Jews until influential Believers entered their lives at a time of personal crisis or in a window of vulnerability. One ethnic Jew found his way to Messianic Judaism through the Union Rescue Mission, a Christian organization that took him in during a period of drug addiction and homelessness. Another Jewish congregant became a Messianic when she fell in love with her future husband, who made clear that he would only marry a Believing woman.

DIANA, A GENTILE

The first time I saw Diana, she was getting up from her first row seat at services, ready to join the Dance Ministry ensemble. I was struck by her blonde perfection. She is tall and slim, with delicately proportioned features, an enveloping smile, and long blonde curls that fall around her chin. When she danced, she looked like a reed swaying in the wind. On days when she wasn't wearing her Dance Ministry uniform, I was always taken by how pulled-together she looked. As I got to know her better, I found out that she worked hard to keep herself slim and at looking so pulled together. On closer inspection, however, she usually looked a bit tired. She had been a model and had learned to hide the give-away signs of the fast-track life she had once led.

Diana, thirty-five, was born in Michigan to church-attending Lutherans. Her childhood was a quiet one. She was in college, studying to be a schoolteacher, when she was identified by a talent scout. She dropped out of college a semester before graduation and left for New York, where she modeled for about four years.

She met her ex-husband, Dan, on one of her modeling trips, and they married a few years after their initial meeting. A developer, Dan was wealthier than Diana had ever imagined possible. He moved his base of operations, and together they moved to Southern California in the late 1980s. Diana now had a house, an expensive sports car, and all the clothes—as well as anything else—she would ever want. When he asked her to stop modeling, Diana agreed; she felt she now had everything she ever wanted. The marriage lasted less than two years, however; one day Dan came home and told her that he had fallen out of love with her and wanted a divorce. For Diana, this statement came as a complete surprise, and she remembers the next few months as the lowest point in her life.

This period of difficulty was filled with "born-again Christians coming out of the woodwork" to talk to her. Because her family and friends were so far away and because she felt that she needed emotional and social support to help her get through this difficult time, she started attending church. Although she had never given up her belief in God, she felt that she did not have the same connection with God as others did, and decided that a church could help her fulfill this need. She started off attending the Lutheran churches in town, but she found them to be "graying, boring, and dead" congregations. She tried Cavalry Chapel, which she found to be "too rock and rollish" and young. It was at this point that she met the man who would become her second, and current, husband.

Diana started modeling again and met Ethan, a Messianic Jew, at the talent agency. She asked him to have a drink with her, but he categorically declined, saying that he didn't date non-Believers. Interested in his stance, Diana asked him about the Bible and about his relationship with God, and they began a friendship in which they would meet for lunch and discuss these issues. At one of these lunches, Ethan invited Diana to attend Adat haRuach with him, preparing her for the experience by telling her, "Just come. It's a little weird, we're a bunch of crazy Jews jumping around, dancing, praising the Lord . . . " She did find the experience odd, but was moved to accept the Lord a few nights later.

Within Messianic Judaism (like in some Evangelical traditions), there is an emphasis on being "equally yoked" with one's partner. It is important that both parties have an equal understanding of the Bible and of their spirituality. This concept also functions as a way of ensuring that the romantic love that arises between couples is not confused with feelings about Yshua.

Since Ethan did not want to encourage such an unevenly "yoked" relationship with Diana in terms of their spiritual growth, he suggested that she attend a Gentile church until she grew into her faith. He was also concerned that her relationship with Yshua might be based on him, and he began to distance from her. But Diana was stubborn, and Adat haRuach's way of worshipping drew her in. She felt in her heart that the Lord wanted her at Adat haRuach; despite attempts on Ethan's part to dissuade her, she continued to attend services there. Unlike her experiences at the Lutheran church, Diana now felt free to be joyous. She also began an informal fellowship with three other women who lived near her.

Although she had filed for divorced by this point, Rabbi Jason counseled her and told her that, based on First Corinthians, chapter seven, she needed to ask Dan if he was willing to resume the marriage and try to work it out. In the Messianic tradition, Believers cannot divorce. However, if a Believer is married to a non-Believer and the non-Believer leaves, the Believer is "Biblically free" to divorce. While it was very hard for Diana to approach Dan and ask him to give their marriage another chance since he had left her, she felt she had to do it. Dan reiterated that he wasn't willing to resume the marriage, and since he was not a Believer, Diana was then free to leave it. She says,

> I really wanted to do what the Lord wanted me to do at that
> point. You go through this when you're a new Believer,
> there's a thing called the honeymoon period, where you have
> a lot of joy and a lot of peace. It's better than drugs, it's
> better than anything you can ever imagine, it's like the most
> ecstatic high you will ever have. . . . Let me tell you, I had
> one, let me tell you, I had an unbelievable honeymoon
> period with the Lord.

During this time, Diana was excited about her new faith and thought everybody ought to have what she did. She fought with her family and alienated them before learning that subtlety was the key in making them understand her new faith. Today her mother has accepted the Lord as well. Diana's involvement in Adat haRuach has made her realize what the important things in life are and how that differs from her previous conceptions. Diana talks about her pre-Adat haRuach self as having been "a woman of the world." In hindsight, she looks back at her goals of having a big house and a lot of clothes, and she is struck by how empty and unhappy that left her, although she didn't know it at the time. Now that God is her priority, in a time when she is neither materially oriented nor well off, she finds more peace in her life than she has ever had before. The first few years she "fought internally" with new ways of looking at the world. She had been pro-choice and pro–gay rights and these were hard views to give up; but slowly she felt that God started working on her and changing her heart so that today her views are consistent with the Believers' position. She has also come to acknowledge her limitations and to understand that wanting to be perfect and "have it all" is a reflection of the material world she was a part of. Now, God lets her know when she is overextending herself and lets her know that she is fine the way she is.

Outside of the Messianic community, Diana ministers to non-Messianic Christians and helps them see that Jesus was Jewish, something that she was never taught previously. At the time of our interview, it had been two years since Diana "came to the Lord." One year after her first visit to Adat haRuach, she and Ethan were married. They do not have children, or any plans to. Diana has never wanted to have children, but she feels that God is "softening her heart" to have children; that may happen in the near future.

Most Gentile women at Adat haRuach compare themselves to the biblical Ruth. Like Ruth, these Messianic Gentile women speak of having a "heart for Israel," and of loving the Jewish people and the Jewish Messiah. For Messianics who are Gentiles, close identification with Jewish culture requires incorporating bits of an alien culture into daily life. Because of this, Messianic Gentiles are often considered Jewish by the secular world. One Messianic Gentile says,

> People think I'm Jewish now because I do these things. And I tell them, "No I'm not, I'm a Gentile, but I keep the Jewish traditions." In my heart, I'm really feeling called toward the

Jewish people, and . . . I think an outward sign of that is
maybe keeping kosher.

Several congregants relate that having the world view them as Jews has helped
them understand the persecution that Jews have faced throughout the years.
By seeming Jewish to the rest of the world, these Messianics who are Gentiles maintain ties to a Jewish heritage, whether or not they are linked to it
genetically.

NICHOLAS, A ROOT SEEKER

In some cases, Messianics dig into the past to unearth a previously unknown
familial connection with Judaism. In other cases, Messianic Gentiles have
long been aware of some familial connection to Judaism that eventually creates or nurtures their curiosity in the Messianic movement. Gentile recruits
recreate their historical roots in order to identify with the desired Jewish
ethnicity.

Nicholas was born in Scotland, where his father was stationed in the
Navy. They moved a lot in Nicholas's early years until his father was perma-
nently transferred to a San Diego base, which is where Nicholas finished
high school. Nicholas remembers his childhood years as very painful and
"dysfunctional." He says his family is still dysfunctional, but that he speaks
to them because, being a Believer, he takes the command to honor his parents
seriously. His parents are practicing Roman Catholics. Nicholas remembers
that, when he was fifteen, a family member traced the lineage and found a
"Jewish line" on his father's side that had existed up until four generations
ago. According to Nicholas, rather than acknowledge that this explained the
Jewish-sounding family name, Daniels, his relatives denied their Jewish heritage and continued to insist that they are full-blooded Germans. To this day,
and to Nicholas's great annoyance, none of his siblings consider themselves
Jewish or are even willing to discuss the possibility.

Nicholas is a tall, twenty-nine-year-old man with short blond hair and
a serious demeanor. He comes across as wanting to belong, wanting to be
included; and because he is a friendly man, he usually is. Life seems to be a
bit of struggle for him, and he is often dissatisfied with the cards he has been

dealt. He works in a home for difficult juveniles and often complains of the pressures of his position. He is very active in the congregation, helping out with the teens, running Sunday school classes and creating activities for them. He is also very good with small children, and at most Adat haRuach functions he can be seen helping out mothers by taking care of the kids; during special services, he is often in the foyer burping babies and playing with the small children, giving the mothers time to worship or dance. The sight of an infant against his large frame is an endearing one.

Nicholas has always known there was a God, but God was not an active part of his life. In high school, Nicholas enjoyed singing and was a member of choir. This membership he attributes to his classmates thinking him gay and marginalizing him. Another member of the choir, one who was also a "social outcast," talked to him about God. At this point in his life, it seemed to him that conversations he was having with people always mentioned God in some manner. He decided to start attending a nondenominational charismatic church with his new friend, who had brought him into her network of friends. Six months later he became a Believer. Nicholas feels that becoming a Believer has given him a more meaningful social life. He remembers the days before that, when he was a "homebody" and had no friends to speak of. While he does not smoke, drink, watch R-rated movies, or go to bars, he has a small group of friends and they socialize frequently.

After thirteen years of attending the same church, Nicholas began to feel dissatisfied with the church's teachings. He knew he wanted a different kind of congregation, but didn't know what. On a whim, he decided to thumb through the telephone book's Yellow Pages to see what might catch his eye. He saw an advertisement for a Messianic Synagogue and realized that he had, in other aspects of his life, been moving toward Judaism and toward understanding what it meant to be Jewish. In the charismatic church, he felt that he was unable to pursue these interests and wasn't even sure what questions to ask. He had several conversations with Jews for Jesus people, but found the proselytizers confrontational and therefore frustrating to talk to. Intrigued but apprehensive about his Jewish interests, he started attending Adat haRuach while continuing to attend his other church.

Nicholas's first visit at Adat haRuach was exciting. He felt that he was seeing worship "as it was meant to be." He was taken by the dancing, the singing and the feeling of "togetherness." He found it stimulating to be able to discuss scripture and talk about what it meant. As a result of these conversations with fellow congregants, Nicholas feels that he has gained a stronger understanding of the Bible and of the relationship between the Old and New Testaments. He looks back at his previous church experience and remembers the dryness of the scripture. For Nicholas, understanding Jewish culture and its role in the New Testament has brought the Bible "to life." As a result, he talks about feeling closer to God and feeling a richness in his life that he doesn't remember ever feeling before. He speaks freely of being *meshuganeh* (crazy) for the Lord.

Since he began attending Adat haRuach, Nicholas has been learning to read and speak Hebrew, is studying for his *bar mitzvah*, and is considering circumcision. (Another member of the congregation was recently circumcised when he became a Messianic Believer and learned that he had a "Jewish lineage" in his past. This move was quite controversial, not to mention painful, which is why Nicholas is still contemplating it.) Aside from the new Jewish aspect of his faith that Adat haRuach gave him, Nicholas felt that Adat haRuach was the first place in his life that nurtured him and "built him up," that strengthened his confidence and his esteem; something that neither his biological nor his church families had ever offered him. At the time of our interview, Nicholas had been active at Adat haRuach for three years and was still finding his way around the congregation. His closest friends are still from the charismatic church he used to attend, but Nicholas hopes that will change and that his primary friendships will become Adat haRuach congregants. He sings for the congregation, but aside from that he is not well integrated into other ministries because he is uncomfortable with the dogmatic nature of many congregants' beliefs. As a single member of the congregation, Nicholas finds that it is hard to integrate into the activities; and while he loves his life at Adat haRuach, he feels that it is hard to get to know individuals. He continues to feel a little isolated and marginalized; although this would not be evident to an onlooker who notices that Nicholas is always jovial and engaged in conversation at every religious and social function.

While Nicholas is single, he hopes to marry in the near future. He sees marriage as the point at which he will start observing Shabbat fully. He looks forward to the time when Shabbat candles will be lit on Friday nights in his own home. As a bachelor, he keeps biblically kosher (see chapter 5 for a discussion on kosher dietary laws within Messianic Judaism), which creates a bit of a sticky situation at his parent's home, where his mother generally serves pork. Aside from his theological aversion, Nicholas claims that, since joining Adat haRuach, his aversion to pork has turned out to be physical as well.

Other Root Seekers at the congregation claim Jewish descent based on a link that is many generations old.[3] Thomas, an older man who brings his granddaughter to services with him, met me one Saturday and told me his story. Born and raised a Roman Catholic, he did not "discover" that he was Jewish until relatively recently, when he read that, in 1492, when the Jews were expelled from the Iberian Peninsula, there was not a single family in Spain without some Jewish blood. Although his family tree indicates that in the fifteenth century his family lived in Italy, they came from a part of Italy that was primarily Spanish.

Growing up in this country, Thomas remembers that his grandmother unknowingly did "Jewish things" such as following *kashrut*, or kosher ritual, when cooking. She always soaked chicken in saltwater for two to three hours before cooking it. She also boiled meat before cooking it and butchered chickens according to rabbinic tradition, by cutting their throats rather than strangling them.[4] Thomas's grandmother also made "those Italian biscotti which are basically *kamish*, and with anise even, like the Sephardic Jews." These practices, along with his grandmother's maiden name, Leonbruni (which he translates as "the Lion of Judah") indicate to Thomas that his grandmother came from a family of crypto-Jews—Jews who converted to Catholicism in Spain during the Inquisition but secretly continued to practice Judaism.

In their attempts to unearth a connection, other Gentiles also find links, however slight, to the Sephardic tradition. Liliana, in her mid-sixties, told me that some ten years earlier she had spent time in Israel because she wanted to understand her Jewish background better. She was raised in the United States as a Catholic; both of her parents were Mexican, descended from the Spanish conquistadors. Their history, coupled with her mother's name (a name "similar to Cohen"), clearly indicated to her that her ancestors were also Jews converted to Catholicism during the Inquisition.[5]

Jewish roots are sought on both maternal and paternal sides of the family. The Messianic community believes that Judaism is transmitted through the bloodline and that an individual is Jewish if he or she has one Jewish grandparent.[6] Two Adat haRuach congregants independently told me that after they became Messianic Believers, they found out that their fathers had been born Jewish but had kept it a secret from their wives and children. It was only after these children became involved with Messianic Judaism and started asking questions about their ethnicity that their fathers broke the silence. Not all Messianic Gentiles who seek Jewish roots are able to find Jewish ancestors, of course.[7] These individuals seemingly have resigned themselves to the fact that they were not born Jewish and therefore are not Jewish by "nationality."

Even if all their ancestors are Gentile, these respondents want to ensure that their children will be Jewish. One respondent felt strongly that her son (who was one and a half at the time) must marry a traditionally (matrilineally) Jewish woman so that their children in turn will be recognized as Jewish by the State of Israel and the family line will become Jewish. Likewise, another congregant wants to marry a matrilineally Jewish woman: "I feel like I want to get my name restored in Israel, because . . . I'm not Jewish, according to rabbinic laws and stuff. . . . And I would like to give my children that heritage."

Chapter 5

Community Building

Tearing Down and Raising Ethnic Fences

For communities that are defined territorially, boundaries are easy to identify. Boundaries for Messianics are problematic, however, because their community is demarcated socially, not territorially or ethnically. To examine social boundaries one must analyze interactions within the group as well as those that occur between group members and nonmembers. These interactions serve as measures of membership as well as exclusion (Barth 1969; Douglas 1970; Waters 1990). Community, after all, is the result of an interactive process in which the community is shaped by its members, just as the members are molded by it (Markowitz 1993). How do Messianic Believers draw up social boundaries? How do they align themselves with, and separate themselves from, Judaism and Christianity?

The Messianic community is constantly working to form its identity. This work entails an ongoing negotiation between Jewish and Christian cultures, and thus results in ambiguities, dilemmas, and hierarchies. A question that arises from this process is whether Messianic Believers can identify satisfactorily with two communities that traditionally call for exclusive identification (see also Gray and Thumma 1997; Nippert-Eng 1996; Stocks 1997;

Thumma 1991; Zerubavel 1991). I believe that although they are committed to breaking down fences between the Jewish and Gentile communities, in fact they produce new fences. As a result, Messianic Believers must involve themselves in producing a novel ethnic identifier and new sets of norms.

RELATIONS WITH THE JEWISH COMMUNITY

Identification with the Jewish Community
The Messianic movement, and certainly Adat haRuach, are stratified cultur-ally. Identity with Judaism is very strong, and both Jews and Gentiles strive to be more Jewish in their involvement in the world. Because ethnic Jews have a stronger claim in this regard, the result is a hierarchy within the group. As was discussed in chapter 4, because Messianic Believers believe that Ju-daism is transmitted by descent, one's cultural upbringing is irrelevant to their definition of Jewishness. At the same time, Messianics acknowledge that Jewish identity carries with it a substantial amount of cultural baggage. Thus, although culture cannot make one a Jew, certain cultural affinities pro-vide markers of Jewishness. Messianic Believers identify with the parent Jew-ish community in four major ways: through language, Holocaust memory, Zionism, and everyday cultural practices.

One of the clearest examples of Messianics' identification with main-stream Jewish culture is their use of Yiddish in everyday conversation. Ac-cording to Markowitz (1993), Royce (1982), and Waters (1990), language is the most effective cultural attribute for maintaining solidarity and integration in an ethnic group. Reviving a language is frequently one of the first strate-gies used by groups that are strengthening or recreating their identity (Royce 1982). For the American-born, the foreign language of their immigrant an-cestors does not primarily represent a linguistic tool; rather, it evokes nostal-gia and cherished memories, and it is often the "silly phrases" that remain (Waters 1990:117).

Yiddish is used in everyday speech even by Jews who were raised with no Jewish culture in their homes. The most striking example is Rabbi Jason, who had to learn everything "Jewish-wise." He says that the extent of his Jewish knowledge while he was growing up was that "Passover is matzo ball soup." Today he scatters fragments of Yiddish, such as *oy gevalt* (a cry of astonishment), *saychel* (good common sense), and *mazel tov!* (congratulations) in his sermons and in daily conversation.

Gentile members have made an effort to pick up Yiddish expressions as well. When I visited Diana at her home, she offered me tea and cookies to "*nosh* on" (snack on). During prayer time in services, another Gentile woman made a plea for "this world that's a little *meshugeh* (crazy)." One of my roles in the community was that of "Jewish expert" because I belonged to the traditional Jewish community, and I was often asked to translate Yiddish expressions. Congregants asked me, "What do *shlemiel* (a foolish person) and *shlamazel* (a chronically unlucky person) mean?" Or, "*Saychel*? How do you spell that?" Yiddish expressions are particularly striking when they are combined with Christian expressions. For example, Rabbi Jason frequently used phrases such as "the *chutzpah* (gall) of the New Testament."

This use of Yiddish brings another issue into the discussion of culture. By speaking Yiddish, Adat haRuach members identify not with Judaism in general, but with the cultural aspects of Eastern European Jewry—it is individuals from that region who are the dominant Jewish force in the United States, and their cultural norms and values permeate North Americans' understanding of traditional Judaism. Even those Gentiles who have reconstructed their biographies to show Sephardic backgrounds scatter Yiddish, rather than Ladino (Judeo-Spanish), words in their conversation.

Holocaust memory is another factor that unites Messianic Jews with the rest of the Jewish community, since Messianic Believers identify with the Jews who were destroyed in the genocide. Tammy says she wants to make *aliyah* (emigrate to Israel) someday because, in her words, "my bottom-line belief is anybody that's a Jew is not going to be welcome here [in the United States] sometime." Kay speaks of her future children as being Jewish, and says that when and if Jews are ever shipped off, the entire family will go to the ovens with the rest of the Jews. She adds, "No one is going to tell me I'm not Jewish. I'm going off to the gas chamber with everybody else if that day ever comes." Nicholas Daniels explains that his brother, who does not consider himself Jewish, tries to be "really Aryan" in his lifestyle. Nicholas shakes his head as he says, "But then, if we get another Hitler, he's gonna die just from . . . his [last] name alone."

Messianic Jews seem unable to comprehend how their people, Jews, who have been persecuted for most of their history, can shun Messianics in turn. Their attitude, expressed both explicitly and implicitly, is that if they, as Messianic Believers, had lived in Germany in the 1930s and 1940s, their Jewishness would have been enough to make Hitler consider them Jewish and have them killed. This point makes for a chilling argument; if their Jewishness was "good enough" for Hitler, it should certainly be good enough for the Jewish community.

Messianic Judaism has strong Zionist leanings (see also Harris-Shapiro 1992), and in their support for the State of Israel, Messianic Believers are thus politically aligned with the Jewish community at large. Adat haRuach members talk about making *aliyah*, and the congregation sponsors yearly trips to the Holy Land. Some respondents have been interested in visiting Israel since they were young. At age thirteen, Jessica, a Messianic Gentile, read the Old Testament and was struck with a desire to visit the places she was reading about. Fifteen years later, she went. Other members are Zionists from afar. Nicholas says,

> I want to see Israel come into its own and want to see God
> fulfill things in Israel. I'd love to see the Temple rebuilt, and
> all that aspect. I'd love to go and see these things that other
> people have seen, the Temple restoration committee and stuff
> like that. I'd like to see Israel just say, "No more of this. Get
> out." To take the land back.

For others, membership in Adat haRuach has changed their relationship to Israel considerably. The Flynns, a Gentile couple, took their first trip to the Holy Land with a church group, but as they look back, they are aware that it was not a Jewish experience. The emphasis, they explain, was on seeing where Jesus walked. "It was very detached from anything Jewish. . . . it could have been here in Southern California, the way we interacted with people." Before their next trip to Israel, the Flynns would like to learn some Hebrew in order to connect with the experience at a more Jewish level.

The local Messianic gift shop carries both traditional Jewish and secular items from Israel; and the Israeli flag, as well as other items with the same blue-and-white color combination, is in evidence at congregational functions. One issue of *The Messianic Times* (1992e) carries a display advertisement from a Messianic gift shop promoting *Shalom Sesame*, a joint American-Israeli project based on *Sesame Street* that produces television shows aimed at the Jewish American audience emphasizing either Israeli life or Jewish holidays with an Israeli slant.

The Messianic Times frequently prints articles about Zionism in particular and Israel in general. The following examples demonstrate the importance of this tie to the Jewish homeland. The summer 1992 issue included an article about a Messianic Jew who opened a store in Jerusalem in 1985 to promote Israeli Messianic artists and musicians. The store serves both tourists and Messianic Israelis, and wholesales to Christian and Messianic retail outlets worldwide. Another article in the same issue, titled "No 'Middle East Conflict' Among Arab and Jewish Women Believers," reported on a group of Christian Arab and Messianic Jewish women is Israel who have "found peace together." These women meet monthly to share and pray together and to study the Scriptures, all without benefit of a common culture—something, they point out, that traditional Jews have been unable to do. *The Messianic Times* also covers the Messianic Jews' ongoing struggle to be given citizenship under the Law of Return. In the latest fight, in 1989, the Israeli Supreme Court denied automatic citizenship to Gary and Shirley Beresford, a South African Messianic Jewish couple. As the struggle continued, *The Messianic Times* covered each installment.

The final way Messianic Believers create identification with the parent Jewish community is through everyday cultural practices. Jewish cultural trappings incorporated by the Messianic congregation include prayer accessories, congregants' eating habits, personal and home decor, and personal characteristics. The majority of Adat haRuach's men wear *kippot* during worship. For men who have none of their own, *kippot* are made available in the foyer of the sanctuary. Quite a few of the men also wear their own *tallit* (prayer shawl) during services. Izzy, a Messianic Jew, appreciates belonging to a congregation where

I can wear a *tallit* . . . where I can wear a *kippah*. Where I can be Jewish, not lose my identity. Because I'm not a

> Christian. I did not become a Christian. . . . I became a
> follower of Yshua, a believer in Messiah . . . and I'm still
> Jewish.

Mike, a Gentile, did not initially feel comfortable wearing the traditional accoutrements. When I spoke with him, he said that he had prayed over the
issue and that someday he might choose to wear *kippah* and/or *tallit*:

> I've been meditating more and more on that scripture where
> Ruth said to her mother-in-law, "Your people are my people,
> your God is my God." And one of these days God may move
> me to that point where I so identify with Israel and my savior
> coming out of Israel, that I may wear *tallit*. But it's gonna
> have to be a very sovereign work of God for me to do that.

By the time I had finished my fieldwork, Mike was regularly wearing a *kippah*
during services.

Messianic Believers adorn themselves and their homes with Judaica.
Many congregants—both men and women—wear jewelry that reflects their
Jewish affiliation. Another integral part of Messianic living is the display of
home decorations such as *mezuzot* (prayer scrolls affixed to doorposts), Israeli artifacts, and Holy Land trinkets (see also Harris-Shapiro 1992).

Food, a very important part of ethnic identity (Waters 1990), is also
reflected in the congregants' private lives. Congregants enjoy eating at New
York–style, or "Jewish," delicatessens. I was taken to such a deli a few times
and ran into two Messianic Jews at another New York–style deli on a different occasion. At home, different holiday times call for preparation of special
foods such as *matzoh* ball soup (dumpling soup, traditionally eaten at Passover), *sufganiot* (doughnuts, at Hanukkah), *latkes* (potato pancakes, also at
Hanukkah), and *hamentashen* (triangular cookies, at Purim). At parties, however, Believers feast on *falafel* and *hummus*—not traditional Jewish foods at
all, and certainly not found anywhere in Orthodox Jewish cuisine. These foods
are recent imports to secular Jews via Israel's mid-Eastern neighbors.

Certain foods and eating habits, including dietary restrictions, function
as signposts of identification with a particular community (Douglas 1966,

1970). As Rabbi Jason has said from the pulpit, *kashrut* serves as a reminder that "we're a people set apart. You're not saved if you [keep kosher], nor are you better; just different. You serve as a reminder."[1] The forbidden foods listed in Leviticus—with pork and its by-products the focus for Messianic Believers, as for many traditional mainline Jews—bring God to bear at each memory of the restriction. For Believers, these dietary laws inspire meditation on the oneness, purity, and completeness of God, just as they do for members of the Jewish community whenever they refuse bacon and ham.

Identifying with Judaism also means identifying with certain stereotypical cultural attributes. At one point during their interview, the Colemans felt that they were giving me long-winded answers and Ned Coleman asked if any of my interviewees ever answered with a simple "yes" or "no." When I told him that people answered in a variety of ways, Ned wanted to know of those who answered simply, "but are they [ethnically] Jewish?" Other examples of Jewish behavior that congregants mentioned to me included being more than ordinarily demonstrative, liberal, opinionated, and guilt-prone, or predisposed to "emotional heaviness" (see also Harris-Shapiro 1992:166). Some congregants viewed as Jewish the emphasis on learning and on having many books at home. Many congregants' favorite television shows, such as *Brooklyn Bridge* (discontinued, to their disappointment) and *Seinfeld*, deal with Jewish ethnicity and its stereotypic attributes,

Messianic Believers hold the controversial view that Jews value "getting ahead" (see Goldschieder and Zuckerman 1984). The Jewish success ethic is another such stereotypic attribute that congregants identify with and try to transform in their new way of life. At Adat haRuach there is talk about Jewish families' emphasis on "getting ahead" or "becoming a doctor," whereas the Messianics do not stress "being a big *macher* (Yiddish for a well-connected, powerful individual)" (see also Harris-Shapiro 1992:167). Like language, these cultural attributes that Messianics refer to are not pan-Jewish attributes but those of the Eastern European Jewish (Ashkenazic) community.

Messianics use a number of elements of traditional Jewish culture, including Yiddish language, Holocaust memory, Zionism, and other cultural connections, to forge a Jewish identity. Simultaneously, they seek to reach out to traditional Jews within a framework that the Jewish community can understand. In doing so, the Believers hope to distinguish themselves from Christians who try unsuccessfully to share Jesus with the Jewish people.

Drawing the Line on the Jewish Community

Although in many ways the congregants at Adat haRuach hold the traditional Jewish community in high regard, they find some aspects of traditional Judaism obsolete and absurd. Messianics distance themselves from three specific aspects of the Jewish community: its tendency toward legalism, its lack of spirituality, and its exclusivity.

Messianic Believers frequently criticize Judaism's emphasis on what they perceive to be empty ritual, and they emphasize the importance of keeping the spirit, rather than the letter of the law.[2] When they talk about legalism, Messianic Believers mean the strict adherence to rules, especially rabbinic law, to the exclusion of spiritual vitality. One baby boomer said that, before she became a Believer, she felt that the more she did—lighting *shabbat* candles, for example—the more God would love her; but she never felt that she was able to do enough. Rabbi Jason, who was present, nodded in understanding and added that the emphasis on doing is a common misunderstanding among those Jews who do not realize that the Law was fulfilled in Yshua. After all, one can "do" all one wants, but it is to no avail if the heart is not right with God: "We can fool people, but we can't fool God."

Rabbi Jason insists that "Torah is instruction, not law . . . we're not under the Torah, but too often Believers say 'Throw it out.'" He agrees with mainstream Evangelicals that legalism does not earn points with God and that Believers, including Messianic Believers, should fear legalism. Rabbi Jason agrees that faith is a matter of the heart, not of wearing the *tallit* and observing other rituals; therefore, when Messianic Jews perform rituals, they should do so voluntarily.

The dietary laws are perhaps the most notable example of Messianic Jews' disdain for legalism. Although some Messianic Believers observe kosher dietary restrictions, they stress that they adhere to biblical kosher rules rather than the stricter rabbinic interpretation.[3] In keeping biblical *kashrut*, Messianic Believers abstain from forbidden foods such as shellfish and pork but are able to eat at Gentiles' homes, whereas for Jews who do not keep kosher, eating pork and shellfish is acceptable (Harris-Shapiro 1992:293).

Thus Messianic Believers place themselves in a unique position toward Jewish ritual that gives them a private symbolic ethnicity.[4] They keep kosher in order to identify with Judaism, and yet because they choose to keep biblical *kashrut,* they end up by not belonging. Messianics' attempts to achieve balance creates a contradiction: In seeking to offend no one, they potentially offend everyone.

The Flynns keep kosher unless doing so would offend their host. When Lacey Flynn goes to her mother-in-law's house, for example, she sets aside the pork sausage from the Italian dishes; but because she and her husband are not legalistic, she eats the sauce in which the sausage has been cooked. In some situations, they have eaten ham because not eating it would have offended their hosts so deeply that they wouldn't be receptive to the Lord. Rabbi Jason told me,

> If you keep rabbinically kosher . . . you can't even go out
> and eat with someone if you're strictly kosher, or go to their
> house or whatever. So I think the Messianic realm to us is a
> good balance . . . it's like we can have our convictions, but
> . . . if someone's not kosher, that's their choice.

Becky, Rabbi Jason's wife, remembers when someone brought a pepperoni pizza to a Messianic potluck; the hosts were horrified at this transgression of kosher law and were quite embarrassed. This incident indicates both the Messianics' focus on Jewishness (kosher law) and their self-distancing from the Jewish community as they take pride in their ability to break down the barriers of the traditional community in order to eat with Gentiles.

Messianic Believers are also disconcerted by what they see as a lack of spirituality among mainline Jews because they consider Jews to be God's chosen people. Adam tells a story about a time when he played music at a Reconstructionist Jewish wedding, a mixed marriage. Unsure about a translation of a passage in the ceremony, Adam approached the rabbi when an opportunity arose. The two men talked about Adam's beliefs, and Adam told the rabbi that he believed the Bible to be divinely inspired and inerrant. The rabbi asked incredulously, "Really? Honestly? What about the miracles?" Adam explained that he believed they had happened as explained in the Bible.

Again the rabbi replied, "Really?" and added, "So what's to stop you from believing that guy Jesus really is the Messiah?" "Exactly," Adam countered. Adam does not believe that one can be genuinely spiritual without taking the Bible literally. He told me the story humorously, but also hoped that I could reveal to him why Jews—rabbis in particular—are distanced from God and their Jewish spiritual roots.

Celia also perceives that American Jews have a superficial cultural identity, that they do not have a real concern with understanding what it means to be Jewish:

> For Americans, being Jewish is like being Irish . . . you
> know, they might even do the *bruchas* [blessings] on Friday
> night, but they don't really care what the Bible has to say.
> And then they come to the Lord, and all of a sudden they are
> just hungry . . . their spiritual self has been awakened.

Both Ethan's and Celia's remarks are in keeping with Harris-Shapiro's (1992, 130) finding that the most widespread displeasure expressed about the Jewish community is the gap between the spiritual and the cultural—the Jews' inability to personally find God in the synagogue.

In addition, the Jewish community's unwillingness to consider Yshua the son of God is confusing to many Messianics. I often heard the refrain "Don't they [the Jewish community] see it? If only they'd open their eyes and read." Many were confused by my lack of acceptance of the idea; often I was taken aside and asked where I stood in my beliefs, given my long exposure to the Word. Nonetheless, the traditional community is held in high regard. After all, say the Believers, Jews are the chosen people, even if they are unable to see the truth.

Messianics claim to be especially confused by the exclusion they feel from the Jewish community, by the fact that the community can accept Jews who do not believe in God or who do not have a strong relationship with Judaism, but reject Messianic Judaism. One congregant told me about his sister, who underwent a Reform conversion after marrying a Jewish man. This conversion, he explained, is absolutely meaningless to everyone but

Reform Jews. His sister sends her daughters to a Hebrew day school, although her husband "couldn't care less about God." The congregant commented, "I guess [being Jewish] means eating *challah* and telling funny jokes." Thus it is unlike Messianic Judaism, which is about God and spirituality, as well as *challah* and jokes.

Part of the Messianic Believers' distancing from the Jewish community is a response to the alienation they feel. While the Jewish community holds Messianic Judaism at arm's length, the Messianic movement internalizes this experience and uses it to protect—and distance—itself from the parent community.

Adam, who runs the Music Ministry alongside Rabbi Jason, talks about the greatest source of pain in his life as being the chasm created between him and other traditional Jews. Although he points out that Orthodox Jews do not seem to care either way, the rest of the traditional Jewish community is hostile. An accomplished violinist, Adam is keenly aware of this response whenever he loses a music student after revealing his faith. Although he believes that losing a few dozen students is the price he must pay for his beliefs, that does not ease his pain. Adam tells how much he would love to go to Chabad House (a Lubavitch outreach center) and become *bar mitzvah*. But that is impossible, he says, because in the eyes of traditional Jews he is a traitor.

When somebody sees Ethan's Star of David, his yarmulke, or any of the other trappings and remark on his being Jewish, he answers "Yes, and I'm a Messianic Jew."

> It doesn't take long before Jewish nonbelievers get it, there's something weird here. . . . You find yourself dropping subtle hints too, just to get into dialogue about it. Like you might say, "Yeah, I just can't wait for the Messiah to come back. *Back*, yeah, back."

Another respondent wishes she did not have to explain herself all the time, but she thinks even well-meaning people do not understand that Jews can believe in Jesus and still be Jewish. "I don't like that the Jewish community just thinks that we're a bunch of *meshuganehs*, that we're crazy, or that we're traitors." She knows she would encounter more of those reactions if she spent more time among normative Jews. As it is, when she meets Jewish people at the park, she explains to them,

> "I'm Jewish also, but I also happen to be a Jew that believes
> in the entire Bible, including the New Testament, and I have
> come to believe that the Messiah was Jesus, and I call him
> Yshua." I give 'em a whole paragraph.

Congregants frequently told stories or made comments indicating Adat haRuach's perception of the Jewish community's response to them. When a collection was made one Saturday morning and individuals contributed money to have trees planted in Israel, one young woman remarked, "I can't believe they didn't say, 'We don't want Messianic trees!'" Shelly recalls that once she wanted to attend a Jewish study group that met in a conservative synagogue near her home. The group was discussing the historical split between Christianity and Judaism. When she arrived, however, no one was there. She called, left her address, and was told that she would be put on the mailing list, but she never received a mailing. Shelly made sense of this episode by concluding that the Conservative congregation "just didn't want me around."

For Tammy, being a Messianic Jew means having to do a lot of explaining. She finds that she has to explain herself to her friends who are Gentile Believers as well as to those who are the non-Believers. Her Gentile believing friends ask her, "Why don't you marry someone who's non-Jewish?" or "What's the big deal about being Jewish now that you're a Believer?" She finds it difficult to explain to people what it's like to "love your Jewish people and them not love you back."

Kay, who grew up in a Jewish community on the East Coast, says,

> It grieves me that they [the Jewish community] desire that
> separation. A Messianic Jew cannot make *aliyah* to Israel
> when they are born Jewish and they love the Jewish God of
> Israel, and that pains me. I feel that separation. Because I don't
> think it's good for Jews in general to fight amongst each
> other . . . even if we don't all agree who the Messiah was.

The Messianics' disdain for the Jewish community's reaction to them focuses on the community's use of guilt. Simon, who was exposed to antimissionaries through the Hasidic community, believes that they begin with intellectual arguments and then work on the emotions by bringing in the Holocaust and related issues. Messianic Jews are frustrated by antimissionaries' use of guilt, including questions such as "What would your grandparents think?" or "Do you think that our ancestors who were killed in the Holocaust are in hell?" Simon relates one of his experiences: "This guy, he started saying 'So you're saying I'm going to hell? And your family, your mother, she's going to hell? No matter how good she is?'" Messianic Jews are offended by the assumptions antimissionaries make. After all, Simon once countered, "Who knows what [his grandparents] thought? Maybe they believed but were too embarrassed . . . to say so." Other Believers noted that perhaps their ancestors accepted Yshua as their personal savior at some point before their deaths—perhaps even seconds before. A noteworthy aspect of these feelings is that they help create strong bonds in a community that is united in its reactions against Jewish legalism, lack of spirituality, and inclusivity.

RELATIONS WITH THE CHRISTIAN COMMUNITY

Identification with the Christian Community
Doctrinally and politically, Messianic Judaism is very closely aligned with Evangelical Christianity. Thus, Messianic Believers have aligned themselves with the religious system in the United States that is strongest in terms of material resources and media opportunities (Harris-Shapiro 1992:351). This closeness to Evangelical Christianity is clear in three ways: their children's education, the devotional texts they use, and their political alignment.

The majority of Adat haRuach congregants want their children to have a Believing education. Many achieve this through homeschooling (see also Miller 1997); others send their children to Christian schools. Only a few support secular education. The Northrops are active in trying to start a Messianic school, but meanwhile they are sending their eldest daughter to a Christian school associated with a local evangelical church. They want to ensure that she receives a godly and spiritual foundation, something they fear the public school system will not provide.

Many Believers think the public school system "brainwashes" the children, in part through the promotion of certain worldviews over others, such as evolution over creation. By presenting evolution as fact to the exclusion of creationism, Diana says, "they're brainwashing kids into believing that. I think that kids should be able to choose for themselves." A common thread of concern among parents is violence in public schools. They thus feel the public educational system is unsafe because of both the physical danger and the values to which the children are exposed.

Many Messianic parents do not support the public school system but feel that Christian schools ignore the Jewish heritage. Homeschooling is common practice among parents who believe that Christian schools do not give their children all the training they need. In so doing, they meet occasionally with other Messianic Believers who homeschool and are part of Evangelical homeschooling networks. Messianic Believers feel that the "godly foundation" is most important in their children's schooling, and that this foundation is best received at home.

Adat haRuach is also connected with the Christian community through the use of Christian devotional and popular culture. Study groups routinely use Christian study guides: the Men's Ministry, the Women's Ministry, and the Singles Ministry all employ study books produced by Christian publishing houses such as NavPress, Bethany House, and Tyndale House. The women in particular tend to read Christian novels, a genre that includes Christian romances. Celia Eisenstadt, for example, used to read secular romantic novels, the kind "where people are jumping in and out of bed with each other." Today she reads only novels that have a Christian foundation. Celia's husband, Izzy, used to read "the boys' equivalent" of the romantic novel, immersing himself in *Playboy* and *Sports Illustrated*. Now, if he reads, he reads the Bible, which he affectionately calls his "Basic Instruction Before Leaving Earth" (B.I.B.L.E.).

All of my informants listen to Christian music or talk shows on radio stations such as KPRAISE and KWAVE. Adat haRuach adherents also interact frequently with other Christians and join them for a variety of events, including Harvest (a music outreach put on by Calvary Chapel), March for Jesus, Christian poetry seminars, and Christian marriage workshops. There are also joint activities with Christian singles groups and human pro-life chains (in which they blockade entrances to clinics that perform abortions). Their affiliation in the pro-life movement indicates their identification with the Christian community as well as their political views.

Messianic Believers are also aligned with the Evangelical Christian community politically, and their political conservatism is reflected in their social and voting patterns. Like most of their fellow congregants at Adat haRuach, the Flynns identify with the causes of the religious right. Harry says,

> If we could get back to [the religious right's causes], it would
> be good for the country from a sociological aspect. I think
> that the country since the sixties has degenerated and . . .
> more they've gotten away from God's law and his concept of
> family that we, as a society, have done everything to destroy.

For some, becoming a Believer has meant rethinking their political stances. Sara, for instance, is now pro-life and does not believe in premarital sex, a dramatic change from the views of her early years.[5] For many, being in the secular world is synonymous with a self-centered lifestyle. Another congregant explains how her political views have shifted since she has gone from "being of the world" to "being in the world but not of it." She says, "All I wanted [then] was just my own life, my own way, and that really perpetrated that type of lifestyle." When she was self-involved, she was more liberal. Now that she understands the importance of being "in the world," but not sharing its values, her politics have moved to the conservative end of the spectrum.

Messianic Believers share their belief in Jesus with Evangelicals, but they reject "bumper sticker Christianity" and what they consider to be "superficial Christianity." Even so, Adat haRuach's parking lot is always full of cars sporting bumper stickers. Indeed, bumper stickers are perhaps the clearest indicator of the politics and general tone of a congregation, as Randall Balmer (1989) pointed out. At Adat haRuach the stickers are politically conservative and Christian (Yshua)-oriented, with phrases such as "Found Yshua" (by far the most popular), "I Believe in Jesus," "Pornography Destroys," "Rush Is Right," "Pray for the Peace of Jerusalem," "Harvest Crusade," "Say No to Drugs," "I Support Our Troops," and "Real Men Love Yshua." The cars also sport numerous fish/Holy Spirit symbols.

Drawing the Line on the Christian Community

Like its relationship with the Jewish community, Messianic Believers' relationship with the Christian community is ambivalent. Frustrated by the contemporary Christian church's understanding of Jesus's Jewishness, Adat haRuach attempts to model itself after the first-century Christian church. Messianic Believers distance themselves from the contemporary church in two major ways: by invalidating the anglicized church and by using a rhetoric of misguidedness.

One way the Messianic movement simulates the first-century church is through language. As stated earlier, for example, Messianic Jews attempt to purge their ritual of hellenistic Christian terms. By claiming identity with the earliest church, they disclaim connection with the Gentile church that succeeded it (Harris-Shapiro 1992:210). Adat haRuach congregants do not deny that they are Christians, but as was pointed out previously, they prefer to label themselves Believers. Whenever *Christian* appears in a study guide text, they substitute *Believer* in its place. This practice of substituting terms devoid of Christian imagery is extended to all hellenized words that appear in a text (see chapter 3).

The Messianic community is frustrated and intolerant toward the churches' lack of Jewish understanding and their anglicization of the religion. Responding in a sermon to those who talk about Jehovah as if it were God's name, Rabbi Jason asked,

> When did you study Hebrew? There's no "J" in Hebrew. It's not *Yahweh* either. I don't mind saying it because I know it's not the right name;[6] there's no "W" in Hebrew. It's clear if you take Hebrew 101.

He speaks in the same vein about the cultural aspects of modern day Christianity.

> You want to celebrate Easter? Fine! Where's your Easter in
> the Bible? These are all cultural shadows. [Our western
> culture] threw out Biblical shadows . . . threw out *shabbat*
> and replaced it with what? [The] shadow of Sunday. But
> don't get mad at me because I use Biblical shadows, the
> shadows spoken by God.

As Harry said, "It's amazing how history's been anglicized and changed. . . . I treasure that [Jewishness] in the Messianic congregation, how that's been brought back."

Members of Beth Yshua, another Messianic congregation, seek to dissociate themselves from "the church" in a number of ways. The primary method is to regard the cultural manifestations of mainline Christianity as separate from its true theology. Members object to "pagan trappings" that can distort the message of Christianity itself (Harris-Shapiro 1992:208). Gentile symbolism is difficult for most Messianic Believers to accept:

> The cross, the organ and the choir robes [are] particularly
> "taboo" symbols. . . .By disallowing such use of symbols in
> the worship and architecture of Messianic Jewish
> synagogues, by calling those symbols "pagan," the disloyalty
> issue [the idea that a Jew who has converted to Christianity has
> gone over to the enemy] is muted. (Harris-Shapiro 1992:21.)

To some degree, Messianic Jews' disdain for the anglicized church arises from their general feeling that the Christian church is misguided. Because modern-day Christians do not understand the "Jewishness of Yshua," Messianic Believers feel that they are practicing a Christianity gone askew.

Messianic Jews, for example, are repelled by Christian groups that believe in the "spiritual Israel." This expression refers to the idea that Jews offended God by rejecting Jesus, and therefore he transferred his holy covenant to the Gentiles, who from that point on became the spiritual Israel. Such Christians are in direct opposition to Messianic Believers.

Messianic Believers also take issue with Christians who refuse to believe that Jesus was Jewish. Believers related conversations in which they reminded Christians that Jesus was Jewish, and the Christians replied, "No, God wouldn't do that to us." Diana recalled, "Somebody told me that Jesus spoke Aramaic, [so] he was an Arab." Her husband, Ethan, laughed when he heard this: "And I speak English. Therefore we're Teutons, right? . . . Well, actually, that's not so far off. He's Semitic and so are the Arabs. Right?" Diana looked at him sternly and gently reproached him—"He was Jewish."

Missy's and Nicholas's comments further illustrate the congregation's feeling that the Christian church is misguided. Missy said:

> I'm not saying that they're any less of a Believer, but I do
> believe that God's gonna call them on the carpet for
> discarding all the Jewish [aspects]. . . . I just feel very firmly
> that Adat haRuach has the best grip on God's choice for a
> true belief. I'm not disputing any other belief . . . but you can
> have a deeper understanding. You can be more closely
> related to the true form.

For Nicholas, it would be enough if more Gentiles understood and did not "downgrade and persecute Jewish people."

All the interviewees reported a long-standing disillusionment with the Christian church. Adam was drawn to Adat haRuach because he saw that people were living as he had read they were supposed to live. He had never witnessed such consistency of faith and action, and he found it very encouraging. Unlike the Christian churches to which he had been exposed, Adat haRuach was not a "bunch of hypocrites." Shelly's disillusionment with the Baptist Church in which she grew up was twofold. She did not like the way the Baptists passed over the Old Testament, never emphasizing Jesus's Jewishness or the cultural underpinnings of the Jewish apostles' lives. She also found the hymns distasteful because they were centered around what Jesus "did for me," not what "we can do for him, how can we worship him and praise him and thank him."

Congregants mention the electronic churches and megachurches as the extreme examples of everything Adat haRuach is not. Billy Graham, Jimmy Swaggart, and other well-known preachers are favorite targets of disdain. At a *havorah* (fellowship) meeting, Rabbi Jason said in disbelief, "I can't believe Jimmy Swaggart still has his congregation. What's worse, the shyster who leads or the sheep that follow?"

Messianic Believers are clear that the one trait separating them from Christians is their lack of interest in the trappings associated with a church. The leader of the Woman's Ministry group speaks about "Billy Graham and others like him," for whom the size of the church and the need to "talk the talk, walk the walk" becomes important. She points out that, in such a situation, the church, not God, is prescribing excellence, just as the outside world dictates criteria for excellence.

RELATIONS WITH THE SECULAR WORLD

Liminality and Exclusivity

Messianic Believers define themselves as having a unique identity that in some ways is linked to the Jewish and Christian communities and in other ways opposed. This identity is the result of their living in the transitional space between the Christian and Jewish worlds. By living on the threshold of the parent communities, Messianic Believers are joined together by a sense of community in which categories that they once took for granted take on new meanings. Members of such liminal groups are generally considered dangerous and subversive by mainstream society (Turner 1977 [1969]), and this itself gives them strength.

Their very liminality due to the rejection by both parent communities gives Believers strength. This in turn results in pleasure based on difference: Glad to be neither Christians nor Jews, Messianic Believers consider themselves an exclusive group (see also Nippert-Eng 1996). Their feeling of exclusiveness is evidenced in Tammy's statement that her favorite part of the Messianic way of life is "the *mishpocheh*, being a part of the true family of God," which does not include normative Christians and Jews. For Rabbi Jason, Messianic Judaism is the best of both worlds:

> It's like I can have my faith and who I believe the Messiah
> is, but I'm not giving up. . . . In generations past, I'd have to
> become a Catholic or . . . convert, change my name, or
> whatever weird stuff went on throughout history. We're still

> Jews and we can live this way . . . and some Christians
> disagree with us. They don't understand it, but it's really a
> worldwide family . . . we go to any major city . . . and it's a
> special connection because of our faith and our heritage.

This spirit is more apparent among Messianic Jews than in many Christian denominations or in Judaism in general. Becky, Jason's wife, interrupts him to add that Messianic Jews are the subset of the subset, the intersection of the two. Adam also speaks of the blending of Judaism with Messianic Judaism, and how Messianic Judaism provides a bridge between parent faiths.

Messianic Jews and Gentiles feel rejected by individuals who are close to them, as well, not just their parent communities. Diana's family thought she had joined a "cult" and become a "Jewish Jesus freak" when she married Ethan. Mike's mentor from seminary days, when he trained as a Christian minister, still writes him letters full of concern. When Ned left his church to attend a Messianic synagogue, people told him that he "was out of God's will." Ned explains that because the naysayers weren't Jewish, they "couldn't understand Messianic Judaism." Another congregant said,

> You get comfortable with the fact that . . . we are a little
> different . . . but it's a blessing . . . in the Messianic
> understanding, of course, we really embrace and can have
> friendship and fellowship with a lot of different people, but
> at the same time maintain our identity.

Messianic Judaism is thus the best of all worlds: Believers can claim to be unique and special while simultaneously finding the community that they crave (see also Waters 1990).

Emerging Norms

Messianic Jews are united in the way they interact with their Jewish and Christian parents. Their relationship with the secular world is less clear, however. Congregants vary as to whether or not they drink or watch television and movies, and for many, the decision to partake in these secular-world activities is situational. As a result, a set of norms is emerging, but it is not yet clearly defined.

As they do with their parent communities, Messianic Believers also rise above the secular world. Many congregants accept most aspects of secular society, accommodating rather than resisting North American culture. As one Believer stated, "I can interact with the world, but I'm not to identify with the world." This was a common theme in services, ministry gatherings, and interviews. The imagery of boundaries as fences was particularly vivid in many comments I heard—"You can't ride the fence" or "If you're not for me [Yshua], you're against me." The idea of being an active participant and making a decision that places one firmly on one side of the fence is expressed frequently: You don't have to "do anything to be [spiritually] lost, [but you] have to actively make the decision to get on His side." Quite a few Adat haRuach members report having accepted Yshua into their lives without knowing that making such a commitment has consequences for lifestyle. They inadvertently "chose a side" because they did not realize at the time that the choice would entail long-term life changes.

Once Messianic Believers have "gotten off the fence," they view themselves as fundamentally different from the rest of the secular world. All of my informants spoke of a certain happiness, wave of energy, or sense of peace that had filled their lives since they became Believers. Many congregants asked me if I had not sensed such a "wave of life" when I first stepped into Adat haRuach. The rabbi's wife asked if I, as a nonbeliever, felt the "life" when I came to Adat haRuach, or did the congregants just seem a little *meshuganeh*?

The daily attitudes and activities cumulatively create larger differences, but some of these examples involve issues that are unresolved within the Christian community itself. The two main issues that distinguish Messianic Believers from the secular world revolve around alcohol and the media, and both illustrate how a new movement such as Messianic Judaism negotiates its relationship with the outside world. An example of an activity breaking down barriers between self and God while simultaneously creating rules and fences can be seen in the use of alcohol in moderation. Some Messianic Believers will not touch alcohol; others see nothing wrong with occasionally patronizing bars. Officially, Adat haRuach is tolerant of wine drinking and tobacco smoking in moderation. Rabbi Jason devoted one Saturday sermon to this topic. "Yshua," he said, "made and drank wine. In the Bible, the use of alcohol is never condemned, only the abuse is." While acknowledging that a sermon on the benefits of alcohol might sound odd to most people, Rabbi Jason went on to suggest that wine brings gladness to the heart and has medicinal value as well. He explained that *kiddush* (ritual blessing over wine) is misunderstood and confused with communion, but that in fact it symbolizes the joy of God's spirit.

Congregants separate themselves from the secular world in regard to the use of alcohol (and drugs generally), even though they do not agree on where to the draw the line. Alcohol is considered dangerous when judgment is blurred, when vision is clouded, and when individuals lose spiritual and physical control. Sensitive to those who do not drink for doctrinal reasons because of their past Christian affiliations, or who are "weaker and may have stumbled in the past," the synagogue offers kosher grape juice alongside wine after services. Indeed, alcoholism previously affected many of Adat haRuach's congregants (see also Fichter 1976; Koenig et al. 1994; Lawson 1997; Miller 1997; Neitz 1987). For them in particular, the issue of drink is a marker of their new life as Believers (see also Warner 1988).

"Not being of the world" has required congregants to rethink many of their behaviors, particularly their relationship to the media. Adat haRuach congregants are highly aware of what they watch, read, and listen to. "What goes in, comes out" is a repeated refrain, with the variations "Garbage in, garbage out" and "If you're putting in demonic stuff, demonic stuff comes out." Becky explains that, because of this awareness, she is a different kind of parent than hers were. She is concerned about teaching her children to put "good things" in their minds and having them understand the lasting effects of memories. The Ruettgers also "realized that there's a very real spiritual element that can affect you" when watching certain kinds of entertainment. As a result, they make sure their children are exposed only to media they approve of, which tends to limit the children's television viewing to public television.

When they became Believers, all interviewees made adjustments regarding movies. A few congregants no longer watch any R-rated movies, although the majority say that it depends on the movie; they have become much more aware of what a movie is about before they see it. For a while, the Colemans would not rent any R-rated videos, but now they look into the substance of each film and find out from others why it is rated R before making a decision. A rule of thumb for the congregants is to ask themselves "If Yshua was standing in the room next to you, would you be doing [watching] that?" Erik echoed this idea by reporting that when watching a film or a television show, he asks himself, "Does this bring glory to God? Would God teach me to go out and do this?"

By investigating the movies before seeing them, the congregants filter out the offensive items. Shelly goes to the movies and rents videos, but does not enjoy watching "junk"; her tastes run to "a good drama with a plot and funny comedy." The important thing, she says, is that she no longer lets television rule her life; the set is rarely on and is by no means the centerpiece of the house. Along the same lines, Mike does not allow the television to be a centerpiece, but rather considers it a "guest." He says, "I wouldn't let some pervert come and stay in my house and influence my children . . . so this TV is a guest in my home. I will not let it pervert my family."

If Messianic Believers' attempt to combine Christianity with Judaism is problematic at every level, it also has repercussions at every level and extends into everyday cultural practices. Believers create a semblance of order by exaggerating the differences they experience between different aspects of their lives—within and without, above and below, male and female, married and single, for and against (Douglas 1970). For Messianic Believers, order is structured around a strict interpretation of the Bible, and they make this a point of distinction between themselves and those traditions that do not incorporate a literal reading, including both nominal Christians and the traditional Jewish community. Both Christians and Jews, they feel, include "manmade" (human) creations and understandings of the Scriptures that interfere with "pure worship and a pure relationship with God and Yshua."

The Messianic Believers' identification with Jews and Christians binds them to both communities ("We keep kosher"; "We're not legalistic") even while it alienates them from both groups ("What's kosher if you mix meat and milk?" "Why won't you eat a pepperoni pizza?"). As a result, the Believers are breaking down old fences and creating, inadvertently, a new set of rules. Culturally, Messianics struggle for identification in ways that Orthodox Jews and Evangelical Christians do not. They aim to identify with Evangelicals, with Israel, with Jews; but the responses they receive range from tepid to overtly hostile. Blessing their Manischewitz wine in the name of the Father (*Abba*), the Son (*Yshua*), and the Holy Ghost (*Ruach Hakodesh*), they succeed in offending Jewish and Christian sensitivities alike.

In examining the contact points with the outside world, it becomes clear that Messianic Believers struggle hardest with the Jewish community's perception of them. The Evangelical Christian community by and large accepts the Messianic movement, and there are no obvious conflicts with the secular world. On the other hand, the Messianics' relationship with the Jews is different because of the traditional community's view of them, not vice versa. Messianic Believers are quite aware of, and are pained by, this perception. Yet their very efforts to break down barriers create new ones, tightening their community and distancing them further from their parent traditions.

Chapter 6

"The Only Thing I Do at Easter Is Passover"
Ritual Worship in Constructing Community Boundaries

Ritual conveys distinctive meaning to members of a group by distinguishing symbolically between members and nonmembers. New religious movements (NRMs), however, because of their newness, have little or no ritual repertoire from which to draw. Some NRMs simply eschew ritual, dismissing it as dogmatic, legalistic, and largely irrelevant. Others meticulously comb through old records, searching for their historical past in order to incorporate it into a new tradition. Messianic Believers engage in a combination of these techniques: They search for their own ritualistic roots, even while criticizing ritualism as legalistic and inconsistent with a more personal relationship with God.

Messianic Judaism traces its contemporary "revival" to the early 1960s, which Douglas (1970) describes as an era of increasingly widespread rejection of ritual. She theorizes that, to most people, ritual has come to mean empty conformity—external gestures without the corresponding inner commitment—and adds that the first two phases in the move away from ritual are contempt for external ritual forms and the private internalization of religious experience.

Messianic Believers, like Evangelical Christians, tend to describe themselves as solidly antiritual. Most believe that ritual is legalistic and runs counter to their concern with inner experience and a highly personal relationship with God. Yet to the observer, ritual is an important part of the Messianic Jews' collective experience. For example, congregants pray before every meal and at the beginning of any social gathering. All Adat haRuach social events centered around food include prayer, and all events end in prayer. Bible Study, Singles, *havorah*, and Women's Ministry meetings always conclude with members bowing their heads and thanking God for His gifts. This tension between ritualism and antiritualism is moderated in part by a constant emphasis on the personal commitment embodied in the ritual observance. When giving a sermon, for example, Rabbi Jason touches on the Sabbath, observing that Shabbat should not be kept in the hope of earning points with God and reminding congregants that "Shabbat was made for man, not man for Shabbat" (Mark 2:27).

Public worship becomes an opportunity to blend the internal experience with the ritual aspect of Messianic Judaism. During Shabbat services, for instance, there is time for individual prayer and a focus on inner experience. As the Rawlings explain, Messianic Judaism holds that the *ruach* (the Holy Spirit) is more important for guiding behavior than are the commandments of Torah. Diana Rawling adds, "We try to focus on what God says. We try to hear what God says for us to do in every situation."

Messianic Believers stress that they are not commanded to participate in ritual. As Perla says,

It's a free choice for everyone . . . there's not really a set
thing that somebody tells you that you are going to celebrate
this, no ifs or buts about it, and you're not going to do this.
It's just that [you're] free to do what [you] really want.

Ritual among Messianic Believers then, is a balance between the private experience and ritual as a reminder and mirror of that experience. Believers attempt to infuse their inner commitment into their ritual practices.

On one hand, the emphasis on a highly personalized relationship with an anthropomorphized God ties Messianic Believers to the Evangelical community and is one example of their common theological roots. On the other, the observance of highly ritualized Orthodox Jewish customs, such as fasting on Yom Kippur and observing the dietary laws of *kashrut* year-round, connects Messianics to their Jewish counterparts. Perhaps, then, we cannot accurately describe Messianic Believers as either ritualist or antiritualist; rather, they combine both elements in observances fraught with internal contradiction.

Ritual operates largely by punctuating life and the seasonal cycles, and thereby protects the observant groups from blending with their social surroundings.[1] Ritual provides a focusing mechanism that aids in selecting experiences for concentrated attention set apart from the everyday (Douglas 1970; Turner 1977; Zerubavel 1982, 1991). Ritual also is an important transmitter of culture, and therefore is a means of communicating social information. As such, it automatically reaffirms the social order and renews collective sentiments. Ritual is also a mechanism by which new cultural forms are created (Gray and Thumma 1997). For Messianic Believers, the simultaneous embracing and rejection of ritual maintains boundaries, solidarity, and identity within the community.

BLENDING THE CHRISTIAN WITH THE JEWISH IN MESSIANIC RITUAL

Although they infuse Jewish ritual with Christian meaning, Messianic Believers have given up an appreciable amount of Christian ritual. Most congregants have toned down their observance of traditional (or normative) Christian holidays such as Christmas and Easter since they became involved with Adat haRuach. For some, this was an active decision based on an acknowledgement of the pagan roots of these festivities. Others have shifted their attention to the Jewish holidays celebrated at the same time. In many cases, it is difficult for Believers to divest the ritual from their pre-Messianic cultural life. As such, there is no one way in which Messianic Believers practice their belief ritually, but the many different practices show how they are continuously trying to make sense of their ever-developing religious expression.

Shabbat

Like the Jewish Sabbath, Shabbat for Messianics begins on Friday at sundown and lasts until Saturday at sunset.[2] Walking into a Messianic service on a Saturday morning, one is reminded of the many alternative Jewish congregations that have sprung up throughout the United States. At Adat haRuach, members greet a newcomer with a friendly face, a welcome, and a *siddur*. People mill about, greeting friends they have not seen for a few days with a bear hug, while children run around the sanctuary. All the men wear dress slacks, though they look casual and comfortable; most of the women wear long flowing dresses or skirts. Many of the congregants wear Judaica jewelry—*magen davids* (Stars of David) and miniature Torah scrolls and *mezuzot*. As the musical group at the front of the sanctuary begins playing and singing, the congregation joins in the song. For those who do not know the lyrics, help is provided with transparencies projected on a wall. Everyone begins to clap; some congregants, mainly the women, kick off their shoes and run to the front to dance. Messianics refer to their dance style as "Davidic dance." Its flavor is very Israeli, and it takes the form of circle dances that vaguely resemble the *horah* as well as other, less well-known, Israeli folk dances.

All of this activity occurs in a rather serene church whose walls are draped softly in blue fabric. On the platform in the front of the church, alongside the musicians, is an ark holding the Torah and bearing an eternal light. Although the services take place in a borrowed church (I was told "You can count on a church to be empty Saturday mornings"), there is no sign of Christianity anywhere. After the service ends, one notes that the blue fabric, the color of the Israeli flag, has been draped to cover the host church's calendar of events, the Fourth of July picnic photos, and, most importantly, the crosses, depictions of Jesus, and other overtly Christian symbols that might offend.

Only careful listening makes clear that this is not a traditionally Jewish congregation. Although Jesus and the New Testament per se are never mentioned, the language is strangely evangelical. There is talk of praising the Lord and of accepting God into your heart. Expressions such as *"Baruch hashem"* ("blessed be God") are uttered in the tone used by preachers who sprinkle their speech with "Praise be!" or "Hallejuiah!" In time it becomes evident that Jesus and the New Testament indeed are mentioned—constantly, in fact—but by their Hebrew equivalents. *Jesus* becomes *Yshua, Christ* becomes *Messiah* or *Mashiach*, the *Holy Spirit* becomes *Ruach*, and *Father* and *Lord* become *Abba* and *Adonai*. By renaming these images, Messianics attempt to exorcise their normative Christian aspects.

Services are infused with other forms of Christian expression as well. On my first visit to Adat haRuach, the rabbi asked us to break into groups of four and to pray together. The hope expressed in the prayer was that more people, especially "our Jewish friends," would hear the word, especially at that time of year, Rosh HaShanah (the Jewish New Year). A woman in the group also prayed for a friend who was having a crisis of faith and whose Jewish family was not supportive. The congregant voiced her hope that her friend would eventually open her heart to Jesus.

To an individual walking in from the street, the services are seemingly Jewish. Worship takes place on Saturday morning, congregants are dressed "Jewishly" in skullcaps and prayer shawls, many of the prayers and songs are in Hebrew, songs are often set to music faintly reminiscent of *klezmer*, and the congregants dance in Israeli style. There is nothing overtly Christian about the services, but they are held in a church, prayer (in small groups within the whole congregation) is Evangelical in style , the song lyrics are projected onto a wall (see also Miller 1997), and Yshua is the reference point of the services.

Throughout the service, the parent traditions are blended by addressing Jewish concerns while engaging in Evangelical Christian rituals, as did the prayer group. Songs in Hebrew deal with Yshua, *horah*-style dance is a way of devoting oneself physically to Yshua, and the eternal light symbolizes Yshua's light unto the world.

The centrality of Shabbat (and its Jewish underpinnings) to the Messianic community was made particularly clear in a letter from a leader of the Singles group, a U.S. Marine stationed in Somalia. The Marine, a Gentile, wrote to tell the congregation how much he missed Shabbat and how difficult it was for him because, being overseas, he could not take it as a day of rest. To make observance even more difficult, pork was served often. At least, he wrote, he was managing to study Torah every day.

To Messianics, the Jewish and the Christian meanings of Shabbat are blurred.[3] As a result, it is a difficult holiday to assess in this group. For some congregants, Shabbat means a day of rest rather than work. For others, the meaning involves Jewish ritual: lighting the candles and having a family dinner on Friday evening. For some it means both. Not surprisingly, then, the observances among some of the congregants who said that they observed

Shabbat were quite similar to those of congregants who said they did not.

I found some interesting patterns, however. Married congregants were more likely than singles to identify themselves as observant.[4] In addition, Gentiles were more likely than their ethnic Jewish or Root Seeker counterparts to perceive themselves as Shabbbat observers. The question of what constitutes Shabbat observance is complicated because both Christians and Jews celebrate the Sabbath. Unlike other ritual practice, such as the celebration of Christmas (observed by Christians) or of Yom Kippur (celebrated solely by Jews), observance of the Sabbath is harder to define because both parent communities contribute to its definition.

Shelly, a single Messianic Gentile, has always loved observing Shabbat. On Friday night she prepares a special dinner, lights the candles, and says the blessing over the grape juice. (Because of her history of alcohol abuse, Shelly has given up wine and all other alcoholic beverages.) Saturday is a time for her to focus on God and "bless the Lord" all day. She used to spend the day relaxing, but this has become more difficult since she became involved with a time-consuming ministry at Adat haRuach. She would like to give it up so she can return to her rest and focus. The Eisenstadts, married ethnic Jews, close their retail business at 3:00 P.M. on Friday, go home, and start preparing Friday night dinner for family and friends. On Saturday their shop, located on a busy street frequented by tourists, is closed; after services they generally spend the day relaxing with Adat haRuach friends.

At the other end of the spectrum are the Northrops and Simon who observe no Jewish ritual on Friday and work on Saturdays. Simon, a single, ethnically Jewish Messianic, works on average one Saturday a month. He attributes his lack of observance to his single status. The Northrops, both Gentiles, do not have a special family dinner on Friday, and Jessica Northrop occasionally works on Saturday. Both Simon and the Northrops believe in the "spiritual value" of the Sabbath and the importance of focusing "your attention on God," but they view these as independent of how one spends the Sabbath.

At the middle of the spectrum are Tammy, Wiley, and the Colemans. Tammy, a single, ethnically Jewish Messianic, takes her Jewish heritage very seriously. When asked if she observes Shabbat, she said, "I try to. It's unfortunate 'cause I'm self-supporting and one of the busiest days [is] on Saturdays, so after services I usually have to go work." However, she lights candles in her apartment and usually goes to somebody else's house for Shabbat dinner. Wiley, a Gentile, follows traditional Jewish ritual on Friday, although he stresses that he does not observe Shabbat "by Orthodox or rabbinic standards." On Saturday, however, he studies Torah and rests. The Colemans also fall into this middle range. They attend services and try to rest, but they do not have a "fancy" dinner on Friday or even prepare a meal at home. Kay Coleman says, "My real desire is that when we have children and I'm not working full-time . . . we'll have more of a traditional family time." Both Tammy and the Colemans look forward to a time when they can observe the Sabbath by incorporating Jewish ritual and by taking a day of rest; they believe this will happen as their family units increase.

In families with children, Shabbat becomes a way of passing on tradition and belief. Many families, such as the Slaters, the Pierces, and the Johnsons, try not to go out socially on Friday nights, but make the evening a special time to spend with family. The Pierces have a standing Shabbat dinner on Fridays, to which a core group of people is always invited. Ilana Johnson, a Jewish congregant who is married to a Gentile, invites her Jewish nonbelieving mother to Shabbat dinner every Friday. As she lights the candles, Ilana "sing(s) just like mom sang. . . . It's just so special to sing the same way my mom sang it, the way she taught me, and to hand that down. It's something that I want my children to pass down too, every Friday night for Shabbat dinner."[5] In another Jewish family, although they do not talk about Jewish tradition, the Sabbath is a time to gather three generations and visit the gravesite of another family member.

Yom Kippur

Yom Kippur, the day of atonement, is celebrated ten days after Rosh Hashanah and is particularly interesting in a Christian context. For Messianic Jews, there can be no remission of sins without sacrificial blood, and there can be no real day of atonement until all Jews accept the sacrifice of righteous blood, which only the Messiah can make (Liberman 1976). The story of the sacrificial goat is part of the traditional Jewish observance of Yom Kippur. In ancient days a goat was brought before the priest, who laid his hands on the goat's head as he confessed the sins of the people. The goat then was set free in the wilderness, taking along the sins of the nation. This, according to Messianic Believers, is a clear analogy to Yshua's "ultimate sacrifice."

Fasting is part of the traditional Yom Kippur observance. Because Messianic Believers regard themselves as already forgiven by the grace of Yshua, they fast not to atone for their sins, but to return to a pure walk with God, to confess, and to repent. Yom Kippur is also a time dedicated to prayer for the salvation of Israel and the Jewish people (Fischer 1983; Schiffman 1992). Messianics observe the holiday by thanking God for the atonement available through Yshua and by praying that more Jewish people will recognize and accept him as their atonement (Fischer 1983).

As with all Messianic holidays, Messianic Believers maintain the Jewishness of Yom Kippur by observing it according to the Jewish calendar and by fasting and focussing on atonement. The infusion of Christianity is evident in the centrality of Yshua to the service. Because Believers are forgiven through salvation by grace, Yom Kippur serves mostly as a *reminder* of Yshua's sacrifice. The Flynns started fasting on Yom Kippur when they began to attend Adat haRuach. Having learned the purpose of fasting from Adat haRuach, they now fast not only on Yom Kippur but also at other times. Although fasting is not unique to Judaism, it has become an integral part of how the Flynns, and others, incorporate Jewish identity. Lacey Flynn recalls that when she had a difficult time with one of her children, who was away from home,

> The Lord just put it on my heart . . . to fast and pray about it.
> So the next day I did, and that very day I got a letter from
> [my son]. . . . of course, He had made him send it before, but
> He knew. He looped everything together.

This story illustrates how Messianic Believers take a traditional Jewish ritual such as fasting out of its original Jewish context and use it in an entirely new way, while attributing it to Judaism.

Hanukkah
Hanukkah does not appear among the feasts in Leviticus, but Messianic Believers consider it a biblical feast because it was predicted in Prophets

(Daniel 8) and later was celebrated by Yshua.[6] This latter mention in the New Testament is the main reason why Messianics celebrate Hanukkah. They cite John 10:22–23: "It was the feast of the Dedication at Jerusalem; it was winter, and Jesus was walking in the temple, in the portico of Solomon" (Revised Standard Version).[7] They reason that Yshua celebrated the feast in the very temple that had been rededicated just a few generations earlier.

Messianic Believers celebrate Hanukkah as a time of praise and thanksgiving to God. Known to traditional Jews as the Festival of Lights, this holiday reminds Messianics of a biblical verse stating that Believers are the light of world. After all, Messianics believe that Yshua was the light of the world, and that anyone who followed him would not suffer the darkness of confusion but would enjoy the light of understanding (Liberman 1976). As a result, when Adat haRuach children perform Hanukkah skits and show off the projects they have completed in Shabbat school (the equivalent of Sunday School), the projects include posters showing "Yshua, the Prince of Light" and crowns symbolizing the Prince of Light. At the lighting of the menorah, the children focus on the Messiah as a light unto the world and all its nations. For Messianic Believers, then, Hanukkah is yet another Jewish holiday in which Yshua has been made the central theme.

At Hanukkah, as with other holidays, Messianic Believers mix the metaphors of their parent traditions. Equating Yshua with light is such a mixture. Another example was evident at a Hanukkah party sponsored by the congregation. This party included many of the traditional staples such as *sufganiot* (doughnuts) and *dreidels* (four-sided spinning tops). In the Messianic version of the *dreidel* game, the winners received framed animal photographs with inspirational New Testament verses at the bottom, rather than the traditional coins and/or candies. The mixture of traditions was particularly salient for me, having grown up playing dreidel; I was one of the game winners, and I came home with a photo of two lambs mounted on a frame inscribed with Colossians 3:14–15.

During conversations about Hanukkah—how it is observed at home and the role that it plays in Messianic Believer's lives—Christmas was always mentioned as a counterexample since the majority of Believers had celebrated Christmas in their pre-Messianic life to some degree or another. Often Christmas came up as a way of saying, "See? We don't do that anymore, we celebrate Hanukkah now." Not surprisingly, Messianic Gentiles were more likely than ethnic Jews to celebrate Christmas.[8] In general, those who had celebrated Christmas in the past were more likely to continue, and those who are always conscious of their Jewish identity have not taken up the practice.

All of the congregants who grew up celebrating Christmas feel as if they have toned down the degree to which they celebrate the holiday. Mike, a married Gentile, says,

> We don't initiate the celebration in our home . . . it's not an
> iconoclastic reaction to the fact that we are in Adat haRuach,
> and that we're just anti-Christmas and anti-Easter, but the
> very commercialization and the Gentilization of those
> holidays don't please us. We celebrate Christmas because
> we're with her [his wife, Perla's] family, and they celebrate
> Christmas, and . . . why spoil their time?

Abby, another Gentile, celebrates Christmas at her grandparents' home and believes she will continue to do so as long as they are alive because it is important to them. She knows it is not a biblical holiday but it is "one of those things that's tradition and family." For herself, however, the Jewish holidays have come to mean more than Christmas. The Montenegros, a mixed Jewish and Gentile couple, give their children only one present each for Christmas; they have tried to make Hanukkah a "bigger deal" since becoming Messianic Believers. Missy, too, explains how the importance of Hanukkah has increased at the expense of celebrating Christmas. A Gentile, she recalls that she brought home a Christmas tree last year. After various neighbors walked past and said, "I thought you guys were Jewish," she suddenly lost pleasure in the tree. The Lord, she says, "changed my heart big time." Missy explains that this year the Lord told her that "Hanukkah's it. *That's* the real celebration."

Some congregants infuse Jewishness into Christmas by referring to Christmas as "Messiah Day." Others, such as Rabbi Jason's family, do not celebrate Christmas with the traditional paraphernalia. Although they enjoy "the world's focus on the true message of Yshua" and listen to Christmas music on the radio, they do not actively observe December 25 or Easter. This is not because they do not celebrate Yshua's birth or resurrection, but rather because these are not the biblical dates of the events. Rabbi Jason points out that Sukkot is the autumnal festival that speaks to the Messiah's birth and is closer to the time when Yshua was actually born. In December, Shelly, a Gentile congregant, said, "I had my menorah . . . or my *hanukkiah* (Hannukah candelabra) set up, and I had a little nativity scene there too; I had them . . . both together."

Celebration of Christmas has little if any relation to a family's religiosity; and children in the family, rather than marital status, predicts whether Christmas is celebrated.[9] A large number of singles celebrate Christmas because they are involved with family members on that day. The Colemans found that a major benefit of moving to the West Coast was that it removed them from their Christmas-celebrating families. Kay Coleman is pleased to point out that although she still sends gifts and cards to many relatives, this legacy will not be passed on to her own children:

> I think Christmas is kind of stupid, personally. I think it's a
> tremendous burden. . . . I think you're either Jewish and
> celebrate the Jewish holidays or you celebrate the [Christian
> holidays].

Christmas, then, is a holiday that is sometimes celebrated at the individual level but is not part of the congregation's communal festivities. It might seem that Messianic Believers would want to celebrate the birthday of Yshua, however they believe that December 25 is not connected to Yshua at all, but is the remnant of a pagan holiday held near the solstice. Hanukkah also does not represent Yshua's birthday, but at least it is a holiday that he himself celebrated, and it thus gains legitimacy that way.

Passover

The public ritual of Passover at Adat haRuach was described in detail in chapter 1. Like Hanukkah, which automatically brought about a discussion of Christmas, one cannot talk about Passover with Adat haRuach congregants without eliciting mention of Easter. Perhaps because Passover comes at the same time of year as Easter, all of my respondents celebrate Passover but none of them celebrate Easter. For Messianic Believers, Easter does not seem to have the cultural trappings of Christmas; they point out that, for most Gentiles, these celebrations are cultural, not religious. Yet this attitude is difficult for most congregants to maintain, and they try to look past the cultural trappings when they attend Christmas and Easter services. The Ruettgers, a Gentile couple with two young daughters, explained, "We have gone to Easter services in the past, but the reason they're special is because of the resurrection. Jesus was the focus for us. It wasn't just the cultural things, the fun Easter bunny and chocolates." Another couple seconded this sentiment, "The little bunnies and the eggs? Forget it." Rabbi Jason takes the cultural aspect of these holidays seriously and says that congregants are free to worship as they wish: "Some congregants have a Gentile spouse, and if you're brought up with these holidays for fifty years, you're going to want to celebrate them."

Wiley, who does not celebrate Christmas or Easter because of its pagan roots, says, "If we're going to celebrate the death and resurrection of Christ, why don't we celebrate it when it was originally intended to be celebrated? As far as I can tell, that's Passover." For the Slaters, Passover is the holiday that speaks to the resurrection; thus Easter is a "nonissue." Mike and Perla celebrate Easter only in its "Jewish expression—Passover." Nicholas will not celebrate Easter with his family because he is "busy with Passover and stuff." Shelly states, most succinctly, "The only thing I do at Easter is Passover."

Pagan Holidays

Just as Messianic Believers cannot talk about Hanukkah or Passover without making mention of their Gentile counterparts, they cannot talk about Christmas or Easter without mention of paganism. Messianic Believers view paganism as a corrupting foreign element within Christianity, not as its predecessor. For a group seeking to build bridges between Jews and Christians, pagans and paganism are an element that everyone can oppose.[10] By trying to exorcise the pagan factor and bring the Christian and Jewish holidays closer together, as in Hanukkah/Christmas and Passover/Easter, Messianic Believers are trying to close the gap between the Christian and the Jewish communities. In the fourth-century, the church separated the observance of Easter from that of Passover in order to establish its own identity, distinct from the synagogue (Zerubavel 1982); Messianic Judaism attempts to blur this distinction. Although Messianics claim to blend the parent traditions, they do so in a way that gives priority to Jewish ritual as the authentic rootstock of Christianity and sets both Judaism and Christianity apart from paganism, whether in the form of ancient nature worship or modern commercialism.

Whether or not congregants celebrate the "Gentile" holidays, they have a collective rhetoric about paganism and about the increased importance of biblical holidays since they became involved with Adat haRuach. All of the respondents, regardless of their degree of involvement in the holidays, used one of these narratives in discussing them. This is exemplified by Nicholas, who celebrates the Christian holidays with his mother because it is important to her. Even so, he finds more fulfillment in celebrating Hanukkah, Passover, and the High Holy Days than he does with the Gentile holidays because they have enriched his life and have made him feel closer to God. Wiley shifted his focus because of his knowledge of the pagan origins in Christmas and Easter.

> I don't believe Christ was born in the middle of winter on the
> birth date of Mithras, the sun god, and I don't think Jesus
> was born that time of year. And I don't like [how]
> commercialized . . . it's gotten; it seems to have left Christ
> out of the whole picture. And Easter is another pagan
> holiday; Easter basically is the English corruption of *Astarte*
> or *Ishtar*.

The Slaters do not celebrate Christmas because it is a pagan holiday, not a biblical one. Both the Northrops and the Ruettgers celebrate Christmas, but since they joined Adat haRuach they have tried to emphasize the Jewish celebrations and downplay those based on pagan ritual. The Ruettgers try to move beyond the pagan origins of Christmas, but this is difficult because "even the tree has pagan roots." Messianic Believers seem to use the term *pagan* to signify a despised "other." This is a distancing mechanism used by other religious traditions as well. Often, closeness creates antipathy and therefore a need develops to differentiate from those that are nearest to ones relgious status. In this way members clarify what they believe by focussing on what they do *not* believe (see McGuire 1982; Neitz 1987).

In the Messianic community, ritual creates a boundary between itself and other activities at other times. Simultaneously it creates difference between those who observe the ritual and those who do not. Drawing on the traditions of their parent religions, Messianic Believers incorporate each into the other; and in doing so, they gain the ritual and belief systems of both. Ironically, however, in this process they also create their own set of ritual behaviors that separates them from those parent traditions. By fencing themselves off from their parent communities while drawing aspects of each into their ritual, they have managed to create a unified ritual, although one with variations among individuals.

CREATING CONTINUITY

Believers use the early church as a governing metaphor to reconcile Jewish with Christian symbols and to create a sense of historical continuity. Messianic Judaism has combed the past in order to create a new form of tradition (see also Morgan 1983). They make use of early texts, reading the Gospels and other first-century works, as well as tracing Jewish Christians through the centuries, in order to establish a symbolic social cohesion with roots in antiquity (see also Gusfield 1975; Hobsbawm 1983). Messianic Judaism is not the only religious community that does this, however. Warner (1988) tells how the nascent Mendocino church he studied used history to create continuity by recounting the founding narrative. And just as Messianic Believers regard Paul (Saul) as having been the first Messianic Jew, so do charismatic Catholics talk about Mary as having been the first Pentecostal (Neitz 1987).

Messianic Believers use ritual to create a sense of continuity. They do this in two ways. First, they claim that the rituals they practice are inherited from the early, first-century church. Second, they claim that these practices have continued uninterrupted through the ages because of the persistence of a "saving remnant" of surviving Jews. The historical evidence behind these two claims, however, is sketchy at best, yet Messianic Believers have successfully created historicity and constructed themselves.

The First-Century Church

Messianic Believers have invented tradition by attempting to "establish continuity with a suitable historic past" (Hobsbawm 1983:1). For instance, they observe all seven feasts listed in Leviticus 23, citing these observances as consistent with the practice of Yshua and the first-century church. These feasts—Passover, or the Feast of Unleavened Bread; Sfirat Haomer, or the Sheaf of First Fruits; Shavuot, or Pentecost; Rosh Hashanah, or the Feast of Trumpets; Yom Kippur, or Day of Atonement; and Sukkot, or the Feast of Tabernacles[11]—are mentioned in both the Old and New Testaments, and therefore are thought to have both symbolic and prophetic significance for the Messianic community.[12]

Likening themselves to the early Hebrew followers of Jesus, the congregants observe many of the Jewish holidays, albeit with a different twist. They observe the holy days primarily because of the indication that the early followers observed them—that "this is how Yshua worshipped, the custom He followed." Rabbi Jason manages uncomfortable practices, such as meeting for worship on Saturday rather than Sunday mornings, with variations of the statement, "This is how Yshua did it." For example, the traditional ritual of reading the Torah portion is followed, according to Rabbi Jason, because "this is how Yshua worshipped, the custom he followed, and periodically it's important to bring out the Torah and affirm our faith."

Messianic Jews are quick to point out that their ritual practice is quite different from that of traditional Jews. They emphasize that their Messianic rendition is a matter of tradition and choice, not of legalism.[13] Given this understanding, Believers state that because they are free from the necessity of keeping any commandment, they are also free to keep parts of the Law. When Evangelical peers point out to them that the Old Testament feasts are full of legalisms—such as restrictions on what one eats (Passover), where one eats it (Tabernacles), and whether one is allowed to eat anything at all (Atonement)—Messianic Believers give answers such as "The feasts symbolize the freedom in Messiah" and "The law is a blessing rather than a burden."

The "Remnant"

In an attempt to give symbolic significance and historical resonance to its hybrid ritual, Messianic Judaism uses the concept of the remnant. The Prophet

Isaiah first promised that a "saving remnant" of Jews would always survive
to assure Jewish continuity and renewal (Bershtel and Graubard 1992:4).
Messianic Believers describe this concept as it exists in conventional Judaism and have appropriated the term to refer to themselves.

Dr. Arnold Fruchtenbaum, a scholar internationally known in Messianic circles, argues that *because* of the "Hebrew Christian remnant," God did
not permit the success of the many attempts through the ages to wipe out the
Jewish people. The remnant is the part of the "nation of Israel" that is "faith-
ful to the revelation of God"; it is the minority of Jews who truly "believe"
(Fruchtenbaum 1974:30–31). Messianic Jews claim that they are this remnant, which has existed for all eternity. Members of the movement note that
the remnant is growing steadily today and cite this as proof of the approaching Messianic age.

While serving as a guest Messianic rabbi at one Saturday morning service, Dr. Fruchtenbaum addressed Adat haRuach as follows:

> Thanks be the Lord, we have more than 700,000 who believe
> today. The remnant is always part of Israel, not separate.
> *They* [normative Jews] may not like it [giggle from the
> congregation], but it is. The remnant will grow and become
> the totality. Although Jews for Judaism wants us to return to
> rabbinic Judaism, the day will come when they'll join us.

Harris-Shapiro claims that the "saving remnant" is a helpful category that
mediates between completely abandoning ideological loyalty to the Jewish
people and the reality of rejection. She believes that it allows the Messianics'
anger toward the Jewish community to coexist with their self-definition as
"true Jews" (1992:233).

Messianic scholars believe that a vital Messianic Jewish community
existed until the fourth century, but that after the fifth century it became impossible to express both Jewish and Messianic identities openly (Stern 1988).
Schiffman explains that, at that time, the pressures from both the Jewish community and the Church "squeezed out Messianic Judaism as a viable option"
(1992:25). Messianic scholars write that Jews continued "coming to Christ"

(Fruchtenbaum 1974:48), but they assimilated. Therefore most individual Jewish believers turned to traditional churches, not to a Hebrew Christian movement (Fruchtenbaum 1974; Schiffman 1992). Schiffman writes, "Because of the intolerance of the times, Jewish believers could not meet as Jewish believers, and consequently, Messianic Judaism had no formal history during this period" (1992:25). Messianic scholars also cite examples of individual Jews whom they claim were Hebrew Christians during this period— two Hebrew Christians in the early 1400s who debated with twenty-two rabbis, and converted five thousand Jews; the Hebrew Christians on Columbus's ships; Queen Elizabeth I's personal physician; and, later, Johann Neander, Benjamin Disraeli, Franz Delitzsch, Alfred Edersheim, Karl Marx, and Felix Mendelssohn-Bartholdy (Fruchtenbaum 1974; Schiffman 1992; Schonfield 1936). From the Messianic perspective, it is enough that these Christian men had Jewish ancestors in their family trees, although they did not necessarily identify themselves as Jews and certainly did not worship as such. However, outside the realm of Messianic Judaism, these claims are controversial, especially those instances occurring during the Inquisition, when outwardly practicing as a Christian did not mean belief in Christianity (see Gitlitz 1996).

Historians seem to agree that Judaism and Christianity were pitted against one another during the fourth-century reign of Constantine, making a dual identity impossible (Fredriksen 1988; Sobel 1974). Fredriksen writes that "the fate of this earliest Christian community [Jewish Christians] remains a mystery" (1988:212). In attempting to make sense of Jewish Christians after the fifth century, Sobel says that there has been no time "during which . . . the movement away from Judaism and toward Christianity was totally dormant" (1974:134). Neither scholar, however, found evidence that a strong Jewish Christian community existed early on; if such a community persisted through the centuries, it was weak and intangible.

Messianic Believers nonetheless maintain that they are not doing anything new. On the contrary, they legitimize themselves by appropriating a historical precedent: the first-century church. This integration of faiths has provided Evangelicals with an old way, and Jews with a new way, to worship.

Chapter 7

Bringing Home the Bacon

Gender Expectations among Messianic Believers

In this age of increased equality and liberation, it is a paradox that many women are drawn to religions supporting traditional gender expectations. Understanding such gender roles is important for two reasons. First, particularly when they are rigid, gender roles, are a way of separating a religious community from the secular world. Not only does the community distinguish itself from the rest of society; gender also becomes a way of enforcing this new identity (Aviad 1983). Second, the ways gender roles are negotiated in a community indicate how they will be reproduced. The production and reproduction of gender roles is thus a means of understanding the guidelines by which men and women live and how they maintain a sense of self (Davidman 1991). Messianic Judaism, a religious tradition that supports such traditional norms, illustrates how groups establish and maintain gender identities and expectations.

Gender identity has long been a central issue for women of conservative religions. Although these women may be commonly regarded as antifeminist, Judith Stacey argues that they are "postfeminist," in a category of their own (1990). They are feminists inasmuch as they have created policies and practices with gender at their core, incorporating "criticism of patriarchal men and marriage into [their] activism in support of patriarchal profamilialism" and bringing men into the arena of the home and family (Stacey 1987:15). They do so, however, within the patriarchal framework of their religious institutions.

Women may be drawn to religious communities by their quest for clearly delineated gender roles and a strong focus on family (Aidala 1985; Aviad 1983; Davidman 1991; Eiesland 1997; Klatch 1987). Such communities achieve this delineation by offering a morally absolute set of definitions and rules concerning women, men, and their relationships. They also offer an understanding of family that includes participation by men in a way that is uncommon in society. Many women who are drawn to Orthodox Judaism are "seeking an ordered sense of self on a personal level: they were troubled by the confusion over gender in the wider society and by the lack of comfortable, established patterns for forming nuclear families" (Davidman 1991:109).

This chapter first examines women's roles in the conservative branches of Judaism and Christianity (see Ammerman 1987; Davidman 1991; Eiesland 1997; Kaufman 1991; Rose 1987), and then shows that gender expectations among Messianic Jews are distinct in some ways from the Orthodox and Evangelical traditions in which they originated.

GENDER EXPECTATIONS AMONG ORTHODOX JEWS AND CONSERVATIVE CHRISTIANS

Orthodox Jews can be said to assign private and public domains along gender lines; public ritual life is clearly located in the men's domain (Aviad 1983; Danzger 1989; Heilman 1992; Zborowski and Herzog 1974). Men are the visible actors in the synagogue, and women are physically set apart from them; men traditionally sit in the center of the synagogue, while the women sit either above, behind, or at the sides. Men's activities center around prayer, study, and public ritual observance in the synagogue: leading services, reading from the Torah, and receiving ritual honors (Aviad 1983; Davidman and Greil 1993). As a sign of their devotion to God, Orthodox men tend to shun careerism; often they give up their professions in favor of more flexible work settings that permit more time for religious activity.

Orthodox women take charge of the private sphere and seem not to serve as leaders in the public religious community. Their role is defined largely by duties as wives and mothers, and they are expected to create the proper environment for their families within the home. The newly Orthodox Jewish women studied by Aviad (1983) had initial reservations about accepting the Orthodox norms, but they explained their acceptance of those norms by pointing out that they were also troubled by the norms of secular society. Although the Orthodox value system was not ideal, they thought it superior in many ways.

According to Davidman (1991), women's appreciation of Orthodoxy centers around the religious community's promotion of the nuclear family. For the women she studied, who were not raised Orthodox, the focus on the private sphere is a shift that occurred with their new belief system. Yet this quality sometimes leads to alienation among women who do not marry and have children. Orthodox Jews marginalize women who do not marry, who are divorced, or who are childless. Zborowski and Herzog state that within Orthodoxy, "no man is complete without a wife, no woman is complete without a husband. For each individual the ideal center of gravity is not in himself, but in the whole of which he is an essential part" (1974:124).

Davidman and Greil (1993) asked Orthodox men and women what they considered to be the positive aspects of their chosen way of life. Men were much more likely to mention aspects of Orthodoxy relating to public ritual, such as chanting from the Torah, *davening* (a traditional, highly ritualized form of public prayer and chanting), and singing. Many more men than women mentioned a strong sense of moral order as a major attraction of Orthodoxy and were likely to talk about the value of Judaism as an ethical way of life. Women, on the other hand, pointed to an increased emphasis on family values and the tendency of husbands to favor wives and children over their careers. Because these religions give men a source of identity beyond their work, they offer women the possibility of finding mates who will be supportive in the home (Davidman 1991). Orthodoxy also offers women new models of family life that coincide with the kind of family they want for themselves. Nonetheless, raising and nurturing the children remains primarily the mother's responsibility. Aviad (1983) believes that the changes women make when they accept the new system are greater and more difficult those made by men. Likewise, Davidman (1991) found that Orthodox women did not mind being excluded from public ritual life, but they would not accept such traditional gender roles in other areas of their lives. That is, they would strongly object to the same lack of equality in the workplace. This may be why the issue of gender-role divisions is more salient for women, and why women are more likely than men to raise the subject of gender roles (Davidman and Greil 1993).

Interestingly, Orthodox men and women both tend to engage in paid work; and often the woman, not the man, is the primary wage earner (Zborowski and Herzog 1974; see also Kaufman 1991). However, even this seeming gender equality of labor norms among the Orthodox stems from men's central religious role: For a woman to work outside the home is viewed as a special *mitzvah* (literally, "commandment," but also refering to "good deeds" or acts of high merit) because it allows her husband to spend more time in *limudei-kodesh* (literally, "holy studies," generally referring to ritual studies of the Pentateuch, Talmud, Gemorrah, Mishnah, and other Rabbinic tomes). Not surprisingly, then, although they may work outside the home or control the family finances (Heilman 1992), Orthodox women claim family and religious community as their top priorities (Kaufman 1991). Their domain is the home, "running it" so smoothly that the husband rarely has any decisions to make (Davidman 1991). The wife and mother is often said "to have power of suasion and of veto in many matters outside the world of Torah" (Zborowski and Herzog 1974:131).

Evangelical women are not excluded from public ritual life in the same way as Orthodox women. The women sit with the men, and participate freely and openly. In some conservative Christian groups, both men and women look forward to the point in their service when they can express themselves in an uninhibited manner, a "moment of freedom" orchestrated and cherished most by the women (Lawless 1988:111).

Although women are the people "of the heart" and have been considered more spiritually sensitive than men in the Christian traditional church, leadership remains predominantly male (Rose 1987; see also Ozorak 1996). Evangelical women are thoroughly outside the church's official power structure. They take the biblical injunctions to mean that women should never have a major role in decision making or teach in any situation where their husbands might be students. As a result, women do not serve on committees or boards and do not teach adult Bible classes (Ammerman 1987).

Conservative Christian women are both powerful and powerless in the home—powerful in the sense that they have enormous persuasive influence, and powerless in that the husband retains the ultimate veto. Evangelical women consider themselves to be stronger than their husbands in some ways because they are able to *surrender* their strength (Rose 1987). They assert that, based on their intimate involvement with the everyday details of the family's life, they have more information, more emotional investment, and often more skill than their husbands. Older wives teach younger ones how to keep a husband from making an unwise decision without appearing to usurp his authority (Ammerman 1987).

In the conservative Christian tradition, men are active participants in the home and in raising the children (Ammerman 1987, Miller 1997). For these Christians, the nuclear family is God-given. American religious institutions relate to the family by providing support and guidance for family relationships, strengthening family ties, or substituting for those ties (Klatch 1987). Men are required to take their family responsibilities seriously and are castigated for neglecting their families in favor of careerism or recreation (Ammerman 1992; Neitz 1987). In Evangelical families, the man or husband is the primary wage earner. Basing their models of family on the Old Testament, Evangelical Christians have developed a hierarchy in which the division of labor between women and men is clearly delineated. Men's responsibilities lie in decision making, economic support, and discipline. Women are responsible for the emotional support of the husband and children, nurturing of the children, and caring for the home.

One important factor that distinguishes Conservative Christians from Orthodox Jews is the degree of hierarchy in family relationships; they have created an order within the family with the husband at the top, followed by the wife and then the children (Lawless 1988; Neitz 1987; Rose 1987). Above the husband, at the pinnacle of the hierarchy, is God, followed by Jesus Christ. Conservative Christians believe that this hierarchic arrangement reflects God's natural order (Rose 1987) and that orderly submission is the Christ-like way to live (Ammerman 1992). If this order is disrupted, the family, and in turn society, will fall apart. Conservative Christians point to the rising divorce rates and the breakdown of the traditional family as evidence of the moral chaos that occurs with disruption. The Orthodox Jews hold similar beliefs about the nuclear family, but they do not subscribe to a defined hierarchal system involving any deity.

GENDER EXPECTATIONS AMONG MESSIANIC BELIEVERS

Congregational Leadership
In the public sphere, Messianic men, like their Evangelical and Orthodox counterparts, are officially in charge. This is true especially of public religious life: Although it is acknowledged that women can, and sometimes do, have a "gift" as pastor or teacher, they cannot hold the office. If they have that gift, it must be kept in submission. Rabbi Jason assures his congregation that this rule is not about women being better or worse than men, but about maintaining roles and thus returning to God's simplicity. The problem arises, according to Rabbi Jason, when "you start getting Rabbi *Judy.*"

Adat haRuach allows women to preach from the pulpit; the congregants feel that it is helpful to get a woman's point of view, but only as long as she is subordinate to the elders. Women also cannot be elders, although women *shamishim,*[1] or deacons, are acceptable. Women board members do not pose a problem because they deal with the material or physical realm and do not minister to anyone spiritually. During my time at Adat haRuach, and still in 1997, one of the five board members was a woman. One third of the fifteen ministry coordinators are women.

Like many of their Jewish and Christian counterparts, many Messianic women secretly perceive themselves as more powerful than the men, but that power exercised with the utmost discretion. One woman stated,

> I really believe that we were created the more powerful sex.
> And I believe that submission is power under control. We
> choose to submit, not because we need to. I think that when
> God punished Eve and told her that "you will be subject to
> your husband," it was because that's her cross to bear. . . .
> We know that we're more powerful. . . . but it's power under
> control.

Comments like these remind one of Kaufman's (1991) view that, para-doxically, women in conservative religious traditions celebrate gender differ-ences in ways similar to many feminists. As one man in the congregation mused,

> Most of us . . . would see ourselves, if you could redefine
> feminism . . . as feminists. What I mean by that is that we see
> . . . the great honor [of] being a woman in terms of rights and
> everything absolutely equal in every way with a man. If she
> gets the same job, she should of course get the same
> money. . . .But we see the notion of feminism . . . as being
> an abusive one that's been sold to women incorrectly.

To both feminists and Messianics, then, women represent a source of special strength. Messianic women comment on their own strength and note that, *because* of this strength, they can give over control to their men. Tammy says, "[Women] could be in leadership positions without being the head. Women can move mountains too. There's a lot of strength and a lot [of] power in being a woman if it is used appropriately." Celia remarks that although women are not officially permitted to teach, they do: "I think that women end up being the ones that teach. That's even scriptural, in the Proverbs: 'Learn from your mother.' . . . I think women end up teaching the children more." And, after all, "Women teach all men because all men have a mother and the mother teaches the son."

According to Missy, the ideal role for a Messianic woman is "to be supportive of the leadership and to also be willing to take the bull by the horns in areas that men may feel uncomfortable with, that a woman could be very effective with" (e.g., crisis, unwed mothers, teenage runaways). The women of the congregation have done this by organizing the Women's Min-istry and taking informal control of the Singles Ministry.

A group of women started the Women's Ministry during my time at Adat haRuach. This group helps women understand their role in Messianic Judaism and touches on issues relating to the private/public spheres, mar-riage, and leadership. The men had had their own discipleship group for a long time, but the women's group took longer to organize because of the need to resolve childcare issues. Although the community is supportive in regard to providing childcare, the ultimate responsibility falls on the mother, and preparations had to be made so the children were being taken care of while their mothers were at the Ministry meeting. The Women's Ministry has multiple purposes: to teach women to submit to the Lord and be committed and accountable to him, to share love and affection "warts and all," and to support one another.

The Ministry's primary emphasis is fellowship and edification among women. As the leader remarked at the first meeting, "We're here [on earth] for ninety years, if we're unlucky. As women, we will answer for what we did as women." During the period when I attended, the tool used for this purpose was a book titled *Becoming a Woman of Excellence*, a Christian volume intended for Bible study. By reading the book and doing the suggested exercises, the women would be helped to develop a stronger relationship with God and, when faced with choices, to make decisions as a "woman of excellence for the honor and glory of God" (Heald 1992:9).

Singles and Dating

The Singles Ministry is also generally run by women, and it is another structure through which Adat haRuach teaches gender norms. This ministry, which meets twice a month, serves two purposes. First, it gives singles an officially sanctioned setting for socializing and getting acquainted; in this way, it is like many singles groups across America. The meetings help individual Messianics to prepare for a future with a companion by devoting study sessions to approaching and maintaining relationships. Books used in the group as study tools were *Quick to Listen, Slow to Speak*, and *Finding the Love of Your Life*. From reading these books, the singles learned how to form relationships in general, and with mates in particular.

The other purpose of the Singles Ministry is to create solidarity among singles who have been "called" to live alone. It is a way of being supportive toward singleness and of making sure that singles do not feel excluded, as they do in other congregations, or unable to minister to others because of their marital status. Yet despite this attempt to bring singles together, some Adat haRuach congregants told me that they found being single at Adat haRuach a lonely experience.

Dating among Messianics is not taken lightly. As in the Evangelical and Orthodox traditions, Messianics view dating as the road to marriage. Dating for its own sake is thus discouraged. Because couples begin to date only if there is a strong potential for a shared future, an engagement commonly is announced a few months after the initial date. At that point, as a prerequisite to marriage, the couple begins counseling with the rabbi. Perhaps for this reason, congregants hesitate to use the term *dating* at all; older terms such as *courting* or *courtship* are preferred. Nicholas, for one, does not use *dating* to describe his own social life. He explains that as the secular world defines it, he does not date: He does not go out with women one to one, but prefers a group setting. Nicholas believes that "you can talk with the individual on the telephone or in the group until you feel you may want to marry that person; at that point you let her know and develop a deeper relationship."

Courting, as the above example implies, involves not only the two individuals in question but the whole family (whether the natural family or the Adat haRuach family). This means that the young woman must seek her parents' approval and follow their rules. Often parents, especially the father, will sit down with the young man, set ground rules, and gain a sense of his intentions. This protectiveness is not limited to girls; parents also watch their sons, steer them clear of "dangerous situations," and monitor their activities and relationships. In the case of older congregants the community often gets involved by offering both solicited and unsolicited advice.

One striking characteristic of Messianic dating norms is the preoccupation with securing a place in the "Jewish bloodline." Christians, in contrast, do not seek out a Jewish family heritage; Orthodox Jews have clear-cut matrilineal precepts. The desire among Messianics is to seek marriage with a Jewish Believer—that is, a Believer of "Jewish blood." Indeed, Messianics have developed idiomatic expressions of their own: They speak of Gentiles with "Jewish hearts" or Gentiles with "burdens for Israel on their hearts." They create gradations of "Jewishness" and "Messianicness," of "Jewish hearts" and "burdens for Israel." No wonder, then, that many Messianics feel isolated and ostracized on all sides. As Tammy, a single Jewish Believer in her early thirties, laments, "I used to cry out and say 'God, why . . . did I have to have the Truth? Why couldn't you have made me a Gentile?' I can't go to Jewish functions . . . can't go to Gentile functions. I don't belong there either."

The precariousness of situations like Tammy's is not lost on the Messianic leadership. In the spring 1992 edition of *The Messianic Times*, "Russ," the advice columnist, states, "The term 'intermarriage' does not, or should not, apply to the union between a Jewish Believer and a Gentile Believer. Rather, it applies to the marriage between a Believer and a non-Believer." "Russ" acknowledges, however, that when Jewish and Gentile Believers court, differences of culture must be worked out before the wedding.

Kay is another Jewish Believer who seems to gain little from this attempt at clarification. She was never convinced that a Gentile-born Messianic would make her as good a husband as a Jewish-born Messianic, and she thus waited years for the right Jewish man to come along. This finally happened when she was almost thirty:

> I really [also] felt that God would bring me a Jewish
> husband. That was something I wanted to wait for because I
> want my children to be Jewish. And even if the Rabbis say,
> "Well, no, [they're] not Jewish," . . . if the Jews get shipped
> off, we're going with them.

Abby, a Messianic Gentile, also prefers a Jewish-born mate, though she cites a somewhat different reason:

> In my heart lately, it's to marry a Jewish Believer. Only
> because a Jewish Believer just has more emphasis on
> keeping the Jewish traditions and the holidays and things
> like that, which I really want to do in my own household;
> keeping Shabbat, things like that.

Abby is being courted by a Messianic Gentile who is often mistaken for a Jew because of his ritual attire, his observance, and his knowledge of Hebrew and Israel. His strong identification with Judaism makes him a "good catch."

The importance of being with a man who has a great love for Israel and Judaism is evident in the following two examples. At one session of the

Women's Ministry, a participant raised for discussion the topic of her Christian boyfriend, who does not have a "Jewish heart." This upset her, and she sought the Ministry's advice: What should she do? How could she explain to this man how important Judaism is to her? The others, sympathetic with her concern, shook their heads at the sorry state of the relationship. Another congregant, Missy, who is a Root Seeker, believes that God will choose a Jewish man for her, although a Gentile who is sympathetic to the Jews would be "good enough" for her.

Marriage

Whatever the preferences of individual members, official Messianic doctrine holds that the only acceptable model of matrimony is that between two Believers, bloodlines notwithstanding. All other marriages are known as "unequally yoked." In accordance with this doctrine, Rabbi Jason refuses to marry a couple if one is not a Believer, even if that individual is a traditional Jew.

Having accommodated to a way of living established by patriarchal tradition, Messianic Believers do not directly challenge the patriarchal definitions of sexuality and maternity.[2] Indeed, Messianic women often say that they learned what it meant to be a woman and a wife only after coming to Adat haRuach. Diana's story is typical: She told me that becoming a Believer and attending Adat haRuach changed her image of womanhood from being "a curse" to being a blessing. She said that in her earlier life she was strong and independent, and was exhausted all the time as a result. Today the responsibility is off her shoulders: Because her Messianic husband makes the final decisions, she paradoxically experiences a new sense of freedom. This is the first relationship in which Diana feels loved, protected, and cared for. The married women frequently cited the experience of learning how to turn responsibility over to their husbands—a difficult but rewarding task for all of them.

If low divorce rates are evidence, Messianic marriages are successful; and like Orthodox and Evangelical adherents, the congregants of Adat haRuach attribute this success to a clear definition of roles. God sits at the top of the familial hierarchy, followed by the husband, the wife, and then the children. One interviewee, a husband and father, said:

I believe women are to be submissive to their husbands.
Again, it's much easier for a woman to be submissive to a
husband who views his role as servant than [to] a husband
who views his role as a dictator. And many times I find [that]
when my family is not submissive to their parents, or my
wife to me, it's not because of necessarily their rebellion, but
because of my not doing a good job of being a servant to
them and learning how to love them the way I should.

Most Messianic Believers attribute the familial hierarchy to their Christian heritage although Mike expressed pride in knowing that his views on
family dynamics strongly parallel those of the Orthodox Jewish community:
"I think there's not much difference in my perspective on family than the
Hasid. The dad, he's the head of the home. The mother's the manager of the
home. And the kids do what they're told. . . ."

Adat haRuach congregants stress equality between husband and wife
but acknowledge that the husband is the final authority when a decision must
be made. Celia described her relationship with her husband, Izzy: "I defi-
nitely speak my piece about things. I don't say 'Whatever you say, dear.' If I
disagree, I tell him." Celia, like many other women, used the term *doormat* to
describe what they are not (see also Pohli 1983; Stacey 1990; Stacey and
Gerard 1990), although "when it comes right down to it, we would do it his
way because there has to be one boss." In discussing the role of today's woman,
Missy said, "I would say [it is] probably just to be more assertive in her role
in life . . . the woman has usually been so downtrodden or told to sit in a
corner and not speak." These women have found what they consider to be a
balance between what they term "feminazi" and "doormat."

Men at Adat haRuach confided that they had become better husbands
and fathers since their involvement with the congregation because Adat
haRuach has encouraged many of its men to make the family their main focus in life. Mike said, "My first concern has to be meeting my family's needs,
not going out with the guys, not sitting and drinking beer, watching football
all day Sunday. . . . My job is . . . to try to meet [the family's] needs as best I
can." One congregant changed from expecting his wife and family to serve
him to taking it on himself to make a home for them and to make sure *their*

needs were met. Wiley said that despite the Scriptures' clear indication that
men are the physical representation of the final authority in the home,
"Oftentimes it's the woman that's the final word. She'll have some way of
getting her word in, and [the meaning] will switch."

For many Messianics, the hierarchical structure of the family provides
relief from a confusing and ambiguous world; for women in particular, it
offers relief from the expectations that the secular world places on the "nine-
ties woman." I heard another theme as well, however: Although men have
the final say, women's voices are heard, whether (as Wiley suggested) through
passive-aggressive behavior or through the assertiveness advocated by Missy.
These behaviors are among the routes by which Messianic women's agendas
are met in the home; but never, as one woman told me, do these women "rant
and rave." They are in the delicate position of deferring to their husbands
without becoming doormats.

Messianic marriage does not allow for divorce. The Rawlings know
couples who have been separated for years rather than divorcing.[3] Abby speaks
respectfully about relationships she has witnessed that were difficult and included a lot of fighting, but in which the couple "stuck it out because of the
Lord . . . the 'D' word wasn't in their vocabulary at all." Harry, a married
man, says,

> What's really neat since we've become believers is . . . I told
> you how afraid I was to get married. Now I've got no fear.
> Just this wonderful security, knowing our marriage is forever
> and nothing's gonna wreck that.

Harry points out that he and his wife have been married long enough to encounter trouble spots in their marriage:

> We've been tested. I've gone through enough that if divorce
> was going to be an option, we would have used it by now,
> [but] we just grow stronger in our marriage as time goes on.

Celia Eisenstadt makes the point that because she and her husband are committed to the Lord, they are strongly committed to each other and "have that

peace of knowing that there will be no divorce. . . . There's no back door to this relationship."

By the same token, couples who have been married for decades attribute the longevity of their marriage to their faith. Mike and Perla were married when they were very young; Mike says of their twenty-five-year-old marriage,

> Perla and I are very different. We have very little in
> common. We are working very hard trying to have some
> things in common and increase our communication. We have
> different racial backgrounds, we have different social
> backgrounds, we have different educational backgrounds.
> We have very little in common, and so it's been a real
> struggle.

Mike and Perla openly talk about their marital differences in front of each other as a way of saying that they recognize their incompatibility, but their faith is strong enough to overcome that. Mike believes that their involvement in Adat haRuach has kept their marriage together. All of the married couples speak of their belief system as the "glue" that binds their relationship, or at least that makes the notion of divorce impossible. For the large number of respondents who were previously married to non-Believers, their current relationship, within the framework of their faith, they claim belongs to a different, superior category.

Children
Children are an important part of family life at Adat haRuach; and most couples there have three or four. Childless couples report that they feel pressure from the community to have children, and all of those I interviewed planned to do so. Although it is widely acknowledged that a couple's decision not to have children is between them and the Lord, fellow congregants exert informal pressure. One couple talked about wanting children eventually, but at the present not being in a financial position to have them. As a result, they are not always included in congregationally based activities.[4] They quickly add that

they are not actively excluded, but because they are in a different stage of the life cycle, it is a natural outcome. Kay Coleman and her husband, Ned, also want children eventually but haven't decided when they will start a family. Members of the congregation, however, including the rabbi's wife, talk about the Coleman's having children as if the day were imminent.

Adam said that he viewed children as a burden in the past, but since becoming a Believer he considers them a blessing. Before he became a Believer he had been married for ten years and never felt the desire to have children. Now he is engaged to a Believer and wants to start a family, and he attributes this change to his new faith. Diana, as we read earlier, explained that the Lord changed her heart about having children by making her realize that she had been "selfish" for over thirty years. Before she became a Believer, she spent so much time thinking about herself that she was unable to envision children as part of her life. She credits her faith for her newfound understanding that life is about having children and being a family unit. Other congregants never had goals *other* than to raise a family as well as they could, but now, as Believers, the "instruction manual" they have been given—the Bible—has made relations with children and spouses that much easier.

Men participate actively in raising children; and they, like the women, try to devote their best time and energy to their family. During Saturday services, men assume responsibility for children so the mothers can dance. In fact, during services a mother often gives her baby to someone else who knows that she would like to dance; sometimes the offer is made without her asking.

Children's names reflect their parents' Messianic affiliation (see also Leonard 1992). Most of the children at Adat haRuach born since their parents became believers have Hebrew or biblical names such as Vered, Avital, Rivka, Naftali, and Gideon. This trend is particularly noticeable among those who had children both before and after they became Messianic Believers. The Northrops, for example, are considering naming their baby-to-be Solomon Joshua, which is quite a departure from Heather and Ashley, their older children's names. This cultural change of norms is far less marked among Jews or Christians, for whom Joshua and Christopher, respectively, remain perfectly acceptable names.

Perhaps the most striking example of the unique melding of cultures that occurs in Messianic Judaism concerns the modern Israeli names and customs that are adopted into the cultural repertoire. Some Messianic couples have given their children secular Israeli names—names with no biblical references, that are popular among Israel's large nonreligious population. Examples include Admonit (Hebrew for "peony") and Shirah ("melody").

Careers

Although Messianic men provide for their families, their jobs are not all-consuming. They believe that spending time with their families is more important than their careers, and they report that they are less invested in their work than they were before becoming Believers and/or marrying. Although this may be a natural change in the life cycle, the men of the congregation credit these changes specifically to their newfound faith. Ethan told me candidly how difficult it has been to learn how to put family before anything else. Before he became a Believer, his career as an engineer was much more important to him than his personal relationships, but now he has put his work on the back burner. Success in his career demands constant travel, but he no longer accepts engagements that require him to leave town unless his family can accompany him. Becoming a Believer has caused many of the men to change the type of work they do—or would like to do—in order to spend time with family.

The women as well as the men shun careerism. Both Kay and Diana realized that God did not want them to strive in their careers. Another woman is sure that if she were not a Believer, she would be "a typical career woman," making a lot of money and hiring a nanny to take care of the children. Because she is a Believer, however, she is convinced that she needs to spend a lot of time with her children when they are young; even though she currently earns significantly more than her husband, her career would be the first to go. Missy, a single mother studying to be a nurse, said, "Oh no, it's not my career. I don't see anything that I do as a career. It's always a ministry. I live for ministry, I don't live for myself . . . I serve God." Celia places her career low on her list of priorities and elevates the role of family in her life:

I used to think that success was money and fame and career
and all that. But I'm learning in this congregation that a lot
of it has to do with being a good person, doing the right
things, being a mother . . . that's a job, a real big job.

Adat haRuach congregants frown on women's employment unless finances necessitate it, but even so, many Adat haRuach wives work outside
the home. In the eight married couples with children that I interviewed, three
wives worked outside the home. One of these employed women works out of
necessity and looks forward to being able to leave the work force. The other
two have children who are grown and out of the house. The two married
women who do not have children work; both intend to stop after they have
children. In general, employment for women is an issue mainly among married mothers with young children.

Despite the formal or official line regarding work—and the rhetoric
about involvement in the paid labor force—a handful of women at Adat
haRuach allow for the possibility of a career. Congregants invoke the Lord
whenever they need to rationalize a less-than-traditional arrangement.[5] They
call on him, for example, to determine not only whether a married mother
should work outside the home, but also what type of job or career she should
pursue. Missy wanted to become a microbiologist; she looked forward to
attending graduate school and earning her doctorate. Yet the more she considered it, the more she "heard God [saying] 'I really wish I could let you do
this, but I have other things I'd really like you to do.'" Missy decided that a
career in nursing would be more pleasing to the Lord and therefore to herself.
Simon, a single member, also looks to God for insight:

Should the woman be the one to stay home all that time and
forsake her career while the man works? I can't answer that.
I think that's something that must be discussed with God and
themselves . . .

And Kay, who is torn between the expectations of the secular world and the
absolutism of Messianic Judaism, comments,

> I don't like to hear the [secular] world saying you have to be
> a successful career woman or else you have no worth, or you
> have to be a career mom or else you have no worth, and I
> also don't like [it] when Believers say, "If you don't follow
> these . . . set rules, then you're not a good mom." . . . It's
> between that woman and the Lord; that's the ultimate thing.
> But there's no formula.

Although the ideal is for a mother to stay at home for her family and not to work, Messianic women, like Kay, believe that the ultimate decision about doing paid work outside the home is between a woman and the Lord. One congregant, a married Jewish woman who has not yet started her family, echoes this sentiment. "If that's God's calling for them, then that's what they should be, and they shouldn't let anyone tell them [otherwise]."

Most of the respondents claimed that their faith is responsible for their interest in renegotiating the balance between family and work, and in under-scoring the importance of children and marriage. Perhaps these are life-cycle events for which changes would have occurred in any case, but it is possible that Messianic Judaism appealed to many recruits because it gave them a framework for natural life-cycle changes they were already experiencing.

When a Messianic family needs help, either because the woman's em-ployment does not pay enough to make ends meet financially or because the husband cannot meet the family's needs, the family turns to the community. The community helps in a number of ways. Some funds are set aside and earmarked for people who need financial support, but other kinds of support are offered as well. Indeed, Messianic Believers take care of one another in ways that none of them had experienced in the secular world.

When Ilana's daughter was in the hospital for a long and difficult sur-gery, for example, Ilana could not spend the night with her because she had other children to take care of and her husband was out of town. People from Adat haRuach came to their home and also spent various nights with her daughter in the hospital; they did not leave her alone for a moment. They also took care of Ilana and the other children, brought them meals, and gave the family money to help pay the medical bill. On another occasion, before a young widow was scheduled to give birth, the rabbi's wife distributed a sign-up sheet so people could volunteer to take meals to her and look after the infant; the congregants eagerly offered to help. The Messianic community also offers regularly scheduled babysitting to single mothers, and older boys and men offer to serve as big brothers and fathers to the children.

These examples illustrate how gender-role expectations within Messianic Judaism are dynamic and fluid, blending both Jewish and Christian traditions. However, the distinctiveness of Messianic Judaism is less about its relationship to Judaism and Christianity, and more with regard to the secular world. Like *both* parent traditions, Messianic Judaism offers a strong emphasis on family life: marriage is sacred, children are important, and home life is considered a priority over career. Messianic Believers seek to nurture these values, which they view as being in direct opposition to those of the secular world. Messianic Believers—and perhaps adherents of new religious movements in general—are seeking a balance between the norms and expectations of their religious doctrine and those of twentieth-century America.

Chapter 8

Looking Toward
the Future

Messianic Judaism has emerged and gained strength over recent decades, while mainline religion has declined as it has attempted to adapt to the pressures of post–World War II urbanization and immigration. The greatest losses have occurred in the most urbanized and cosmopolitan churches, those stressing individualism and pluralism in belief (Finke and Stark 1992; Kelley 1972; Roof and McKinney 1988). Mainstream Judaism has also declined in membership since the 1950s, particularly those branches that share traits with the hardest-hit Protestant churches (Roof and McKinney 1988). At the same time, Messianic Judaism is flourishing alongside other Evangelical groups. These growing conservative Christian organizations differ from their liberal counterparts in their distinctive beliefs and moral teachings; they offer an experiential faith centered around belief in salvation through personal commitment to Jesus.

Nascent evangelical groups, like Messianic Judaism, offer strongly conservative doctrines, personal forms of worship, and the promise of salvation and redemption—in short, a clear identity in a shifting world (Miller 1997; Perrin and Mauss 1991; Warner 1988). Messianic Believers' tight community boundaries contrast sharply with the doctrinal "fuzziness" of mainstream liberal churches. In response to their parent communities, however, which draw sharp distinctions between themselves, Messianic Believers have tried to make those distinctions "fuzzy." Yet their fluidity and fuzziness does not reach past the Evangelical and Jewish cultures; Messianic Judaism is firmly bounded vis-à-vis secular society. Messianics are absolutely clear as to who is within the group and who is not.

According to Zerubavel (1991), those who have the ability to be both rigid and fuzzy are "flexible." By recognizing structure and feeling comfortable destroying it, the flexible mind recognizes that any entity can be situated in more than one context. Flexibility implies that the symbols and meanings of a cultural group are dynamic. While they still carve up the world into categories (Believers versus non-Believers) Messianic Believers' religious expression is dynamic, always in flux, and open to negotiation at the level of the individual and at the level of the movement itself. Not only does Messianic Judaism give adherents answers to their spiritual questions, but it provides "distinctiveness;" it is different from other religious communities because of its moral and spiritual codes. Marty says it best when he writes about these groups that, "on the one hand, they provide meaning, belonging, and identity apparently *over against* other Americans while on the other hand they are taught to *fit in with the other Americans* to be the real and true citizens" (1976:105).

"Distinctiveness" is perhaps best understood when thinking about its ethnic dimension. Ethnic religion provides a sense of a collective experience, a sense of participating in the same community with a past and a future (Gusfield 1975). Ethnicity provides a commitment that grounds the collectivity and increases social cohesion (Hall 1988). There are many ways in which a group can maintain strong boundaries and high degrees of member commitment and construct a distinct identity vis-à-vis dominant middle-class American white culture (Hall 1988; Hirschman 1970; Marty 1976).

Dynamic boundaries make for a cultural tradition that is ever changing, "an ongoing dialogue among people and traditions" (Markowitz 1993:6). According to Nippert-Eng, "boundary work" is "enacted and enhanced through a visible collection of activities that help reinforce distinctions" (1996:6). Examples of these activities are the clothes, foods, language, and memories that Messianic Believers draw upon. Therefore, the production of boundaries is communally constructed (see Nagel 1994).

Just as Messianic Judaism constructs its boundaries, Messianic Believers also are creatively integrating and restructuring their identities (see also Feher 1998; Kurien 1998; Thumma 1991; Stokes 1997). This is not surprising in light of findings by Waters (1990) and Nagel (1994). The struggle between two poles, individualism and community, results in a flexible ethnicity (Waters 1990). Part of the appeal Messianic Judaism has for recruits is the ethnic "status" conferred by their identification as Jews: Being ethnic makes people feel unique and special while giving them a sense of belonging to a collectivity. Being Jewish, or having "a Jewish heart," symbolizes a permanence that cannot be severed, that cannot eradicate Jewish identity (Markowitz 1993). The symbolic ethnicity of Messianic Judaism gives individuals a sense of conformity, but with the element of choice. It allows Messianic Believers to feel unique without individual cost.

Messianic Judaism provides a sense of morality, of right and wrong, that many adherents at Adat haRuach feel is missing from "anything-goes liberalism [religion]." It does so with a style of worship that is "freeing," in refreshing contrast to that of the religious institutions from which the large majority of Messianic Believers come. Messianic services are joyful; singing and dancing are part of the experience, and there is an effusive vitality that is rarely felt in mainline synagogues or churches. Messianic Judaism has renewed a spontaneous style of worship among Gentiles that takes them back to the roots of their faith since Messianics believe that Gentiles worshipped in this way historically.

Adherents of Messianic Judaism reason that their denomination attracts Jews because of its familiarity and Gentiles because of its authenticity and historicity. For Jews, Messianic Judaism allows a personal relationship with God; it permits them to integrate their faith in Jesus with their Jewish identity. Alienated from their families and from the traditional Jewish communities, these people have found something that resonates with their childhood experiences and allows them to hold on to their Jewishness, an important aspect of their identity (see also Kohn 1987). Most Jewish congregants at Adat haRuach said something to the effect that "before Messianic Judaism, I thought that once I became a Christian, I was automatically no longer a Jew." Being a Messianic, they say, has strengthened their Jewish identity. By establishing a personal relationship with God, Messianic Believers have transcended what some people call the "greeting card" version of Judaism. Many feel that becoming Messianic Believers was a sort of homecoming, that they were "returning" to that from which they had strayed; they report that they feel more Jewish now than ever before.

The congregants show a distinctive trend toward increased Jewishness: Those who grew up Jewish now value their heritage more fully; others are pleased to discover that they are Jewish; still others continue to dig through their ancestral past in hopes of finding a connection to the "Chosen People." Messianic Judaism has given Believers not only a sense of ethnicity and community, but also the feeling that they *belong* to an ethnic community. Once they become Messianic Believers, Gentiles as well as Jews emphasize their ties to the Jewish community and create a hierarchy that places ethnic Jews at the top. Although Messianic theology teaches that Jews remain Jews and Gentiles remain Gentiles, in practice the actual distinction is not so clear-cut. At Adat haRuach, the dividing line between ethnic Jews and Gentiles is fuzzy, creating yet new layers within an already complex hierarchy.

This interest in developing a Jewish ethnic identity may not be surprising when we consider the 1960s, when Messianic Judaism arose. At that time, in American Judaism specifically, people began increasingly to identify with their ethnic heritage. At the same time, they began to rethink their religious options and modes of worship. This situation was fertile ground for the growth of Messianic Judaism.[1]

All of the congregants interviewed at Adat haRuach had been in search of a personal identity—they had all been "looking for something"—before their born-again experience (see also Danzger 1989; Neitz 1987). Some were responding to a specific crisis in their lives; others, to a search for God. Some found Evangelical Christianity and/or Messianic Judaism immediately. Others picked their way through the New Age, yogic philosophy, meditation, Alcoholics Anonymous, and Eastern religions before arriving at Messianic Judaism as their answer. Perhaps some are still seeking. Most of my informants had tried a number of Evangelical Christian churches before they became involved with Adat haRuach.

Messianic Judaism combines religion and ethnicity in a novel way. In general, the ability of an ethnic group to maintain its identity and survive as a distinct group may depend on its ability to develop meaningful symbols.

Cultural constructions assist in constructing community when they define the boundaries of collective identity, establish membership criteria, generate a shared symbolic vocabulary, and define a common purpose (Nagel 1994:163; see also Nipert-Eng 1996). The Messianic movement has done this by drawing on symbols from both parent communities and, in the process, it has created its own. Messianic Believers are engaged in "culture work" (see Becker 1994) because they are involved in creating agency and intention by mining their parent traditions for ideas and symbols and stories. While the process is creative, it takes place in the context of the Messianic repertoire of institutionalized understandings and symbolic representations.

By adopting the religious codes of mainstream parent communities, a new group, in some ways, is creating and perpetuating the social structure—granted, with a twist. Messianic Judaism did not develop "out of the blue"; it has a historical development that is aided by the rhetoric of the movement itself. Gaining strength during a time of American ethnic revitalization, it has continued to adapt and form itself in relation to its parent communities.

The collective community of Messianic Judaism in general, and of Adat haRuach in particular, provides the congregation with one set of texts. These are paralleled by the texts of the individuals and families. The collective story gives individuals free rein in constructing a working definition of Messianic Judaism as it applies to their daily and personal lives. Consistencies exist, as well as great variation in the way congregants order their lives. Thus, for example, although the basic theological understanding of certain holidays is clear, individuals find many different ways of celebrating them in their own homes; some disdain Christmas, while others set up trees in their living rooms, for example. Likewise, gender roles in the community are widely understood: The order of hierarchy is Yshua, the man, and then his wife. Yet individuals makes sense of this hierarchy in many ways in their daily lives. Does this variability mean that the institutional framework is ineffective? Or does the movement gain strength from the fact that it allows variation among its followers? To understand Messianic Believers we can examine how they have discovered and forged religio-ethnic identities based on their strategies of action. That is, their identity does not precede action (see Swidler 1986). Rather, Messianic Believers have developed an array of action strategies, within certain boundaries.

Messianic Believers are between two social worlds: the worlds of Evangelicalism and of Judaism. Messianics consider themselves a continuation of both, a bridge that joins the two traditions. Both parent traditions, however, view them as apostates. For the Messianics themselves, this transitional space between worlds is bounded by ritual that separates them from their parent communities and segregates them unto themselves (see also Turner 1969, 1987). Thus, Messianics are considered marginal by the normative Jewish community, to whom they represent a symbolic threat. They are a threat not because they are Christian but because they refuse to recognize the Jewish/Christian boundary. Messianics blur the categories that make the Jewish community comfortable and, therefore, become "dangerous" (Douglas 1970). To those who wonder whether Messianic Believers are Jews, I can only say that we must think about what we mean by being Jewish. In terms of ethnicity, they are more culturally Jewish and more proud of their Jewish heritage than many mainstream Jews; certainly more so than JUBUs (Jewish Buddists) and other Jews who join NRMs that are not Christian and yet are not ostracized by the Jewish community.

To many Evangelicals who are familiar and comfortable with ethnic Christians, Messianics are not "dangerous." Messianic Believers fall under a large umbrella where all "Bible-Believers" are "Brothers in Christ," and therefore related. To Evangelicals, Messianics are outside the mainstream but still definable. This point is made by Rabbi Jason in sermons, when he compares Jewish Christians to members of the Hispanic, Vietnamese, Korean, African-American, and Japanese churches, explaining that they are all Bible-believing (e.g. Evangelical) churches even if "they eat sushi and we eat bagels." Like all of these cultural groups, Messianic Believers view themselves as a Jewish ethnic group within the "larger body of Christ."

Perhaps one could have predicted that the Hebrew Christian movement, along its path towards Judaization, would cease calling itself Christian at all, as the Messianics have done. Perhaps one also could have predicted that ultimately they would reembrace their Jewish heritage and begin identifying as Jews. The question now, however, is if Messianic Judaism is as Judaized as any Hebrew Christian movement can ever become, or whether it is merely the latest stage in the Jewish Christian struggle for self-definition.

AFTERWORD

What will be the next step for Messianic Judaism? The most intriguing question is whether it will ever gain acceptance alongside other Jewish denominations, which themselves met with strong initial resistance. This was, for example, the experience of the now-mainline Reform movement when it emerged in the 1880s. If the vehement rejection by mainstream Jews continues, it may push the Messianic movement back toward the Evangelical fold. Historically, most Hebrew Christians were absorbed, rather anonymously, into the larger Christian community. Today the conventional understanding that one cannot simultaneously be Christian and Jewish persists, making the normative Jewish community's acceptance of Messianic Judaism unlikely. And yet, normative Judaism could use the example of Messianic Judaism's success to revitalize itself by understanding what this new tradition offers that mainstream Judaism does not.

Five years after my fieldwork, many changes have taken place at Adat haRuach. Of the ten individuals and ten couples I interviewed, four individuals and five couples have left the congregation. For the Eisenstadts and for Simon, Adat haRuach did not have a strong enough "Messianic vision." Frustrated by seeing how much the congregation caters to the Gentiles, they left in search of a "more Jewish" service. Others left not because they were frustrated with Adat haRuach's level of Judaism, but because they felt they needed to increase their personal involvement with Jewishness. Nicholas left Southern California for the East Coast, where he spent a summer at an American Board of Missions to the Jews–sponsored program learning how best to evangelize to Jews. He has resettled in New York City so that he can live among a larger concentration of Jews and can witness more effectively to the Jewish community. Gabe Montenegro resigned from his job in El Leon and moved to Israel, with his wife, Sara, and their children. He has found work there in a Christian organization, and he is happy to be making his life among Jews in the Holy Land.

Others, however, left because they found the degree of Jewish expression at Adat haRuach exaggerated and stifling. The Northrops decided to leave when they suggested to the music committee that the congregation sing a particular song—one that contained a passing reference to Yshua as "Christ." When the rabbi pointed out that this mention might turn mainline Jews away, the Northrops decided that they had had enough of Judaism to the exclusion of the Gentile culture in which they had grown up.

Still others left the community because of its strong social control. For the Flynns, the "family" atmosphere that initially had attracted them to Adat haRuach became overwhelming: They felt overextended and taken for granted. When Lacey Flynn was asked to travel on behalf of the congregation against her husband's wishes, she felt that the congregation's priorities were out of line, and the couple left the congregation. Similarly, the Pierces left when they felt they were not receiving recognition for their contributions of time, energy, and talent to the congregation.

The rest of my informants stay at Adat haRuach because of the family feeling. When Ilana packed her bags to separate from her husband, the entire congregation became involved. They stopped her from leaving him while giving the couple the emotional support they needed to work out their problems. Ilana knows that this kind of help and concern cannot be found elsewhere and credits Adat haRuach with her and her husband's ability to work out their problems. (Not all couples are this "lucky." The Ruettgers marriage has disintegrated.) Kay Coleman, too, is grateful for the congregation's support. When her husband, an active Adat haRuach participant, left her (a year after our interview), she was still welcome at Adat haRuach. She thanks her "Adat family" for having helped and supported her through yet another rough period in her life. Tammy, Abby, and Wiley also continue to enjoy that "family feel"—they have all married fellow Messianic congregants in the last three years.

The unfolding of these individual lives sheds light on the issues facing Messianic Judaism: In its attempts at Judaizing, it has left behind those for whom Adat haRuach is not Jewish enough and those for whom it is too Jewish. In its high degree of social control, it has retained (and certainly attracted) some congregants while sending others back to their search for a spirituality and/or a (congregational) fellowship that better fits their needs. What will become of the first-born generation of Messianic Jews now coming of age? Will the movement loosen its grip and become less strict, going the way of low-tension mainline religions? Or will it find a balance? Or will the constant negotiation keep the movement alive? Perhaps it is a waystation where people work out their identities or a more stable niche.

What does the future of Messianic Judaism hold for those growing up in the tradition who no longer draw on their Jewish and Christian backgrounds, but whose cultural toolkit was created by previous Messianics? As America's religious and ethnic trends continue to unfold, Messianic Jews no doubt will find themselves struggling to maintain a foothold on rapidly shifting ground.

Making Contact and Taking Part
Methodology

Since congregations are a place where religious and social needs are met, where people can gather for communal expression and emotional, spiritual, and practical support, they offer the ideal canvas for studying issues of religious identity. Such a study creates the opportunity to flesh out issues of a nature that can only be gotten at through face-to-face interaction and by observing relationships over time; this is especially true for those congregations, like Messianic Judaism, who are accused of stealth, of "pretending" they are Jewish in order to attract adherents. Spending extended periods of time with a congregation allows the ethnographer to watch and engage in relationships and see beyond the veneer.

When I started my fieldwork at Adat haRuach, I did not know anyone in the congregation. Perhaps naively, I had not made contact with Adat haRuach's Messianic rabbi, Jason Slater. His initial hesitancy to let me participate was very understandable, given the movement's history with the Jewish community and with Jewish antimissionary groups. The congregation had had some unpleasant experiences, both with the Jewish press and with Jewish individuals. For all he knew, I was a Jew who would "make trouble."

When I first met with Rabbi Jason, he asked me many questions about who I was and what my intentions were. He wanted to know how open I was to the movement. I offered to bring a letter of introduction from my dissertation advisor, and Rabbi Jason readily accepted. I further assuaged his doubts by explaining that I would fictionalize the congregants' names as well as the name and location of the congregation itself. By the end of our meeting, the rabbi said he would be happy to have me there. He felt I could help clear some misconceptions about the movement, but he said that the board of the congregation had the final say. After receiving the letter of introduction from my advisor, the board agreed to my participation.

In order to become as involved as possible, I became a participant observer. I was always aware of my outsider status, yet I came to feel like a welcome member in the congregation. I had not made the "leap of faith" that the congregants had, thus it was not possible for me to understand fully what they were thinking and feeling at any given time. Instead of trying to think and feel as they did, I attempted, by observing my own reactions, to understand how a newcomer might be taken into a community such as this one. In this way, I was able to develop a reading on how young Jews like me are embraced. With my antennae up, I settled in and started asking questions.

I began by attending every event open to congregants. Whenever the congregation doors or people's homes were open, I was there. These events included weekly services, Women's Ministry, Bible study, and the bimonthly *havorah*, as well as social functions ranging from birthdays and lunch dates to consecrations and Shabbat dinners. I was excluded only from those events that were open only to members, primarily board events. Certainly it would have been fruitful to have this "in," but since the majority of congregants was also excluded, I was not marginalized by these sessions. The other events that I did not attend were the men's groups. Although conceivably I might have been allowed an occasional visit, I felt that even making the request might jeopardize my position. After all, I was at Adat haRuach not only as a researcher, but also as a young woman. By the end of my stay, some of these restrictions had been lifted informally. When the organizer of a camping trip asked if I would participate, I asked if I could do so as a non-Believer. "Sure!" he answered. "You've been hanging around us long enough."

My official introduction to the community was a result of requesting Rabbi Jason's help on the next stage of the project. I was preparing to conduct in-depth interviews; the rabbi helped me in my selection of subjects, and approved and offered suggestions on the final questionnaire. I interviewed twenty sets of people: ten single congregants and ten couples. Half were Jewish, the other half Gentile. Half of them were members of the congregation; the other half attended Adat haRuach regularly but had not officially joined. I tape-recorded each interview and took notes as the respondent talked.

Up to this point, I had been taking notes at all the events. This was easy during services and related study groups because many people either took notes or wrote in or highlighted text in their Bibles. Although my note taking was relatively inconspicuous, people teased me about it. The teasing took various forms—looking over my shoulder to see what I found worthy of documentation; asking me if I had "got that down," or "Shouldn't you be taking notes?", inquiring after the whereabouts of my yellow pad when it was not in full view; giving me nicknames such as "the woman with the attached notebook." A small group of congregants referred to me affectionately as "the spy."

As is typical of this work, my interview protocol changed over time. As I began to second-guess the answers to certain questions successfully, I found myself wondering how I could change the questions to avoid receiving "packaged" answers. Perhaps more importantly, the initial question I had posed for myself—"How do Jews reconcile their Judaism with their new-found Christian identity?"—began to change as I found that most adherents were actually trying to Judaize Christianity or to Judaize their own somewhat secular Jewish identity. In other words, my ethnographic work shed light on a whole set of cultural issues whose existence I had not suspected previously (see also Nippert-Eng 1996).

People generally were quite willing to be interviewed. Of the people I approached, only one person refused, on the grounds that there was too much emotional confusion in her life at the time. Two couples agreed to be interviewed, but then were too busy to set a meeting. One of these couples confided much later that they felt uncomfortable talking about Messianic Judaism until they had worked out their own mixed feelings about the congregation and the movement.

I conducted the interviews at the locations of the respondents' choice. I interviewed all of the couples in their own homes, many of them over dinner. While I was obliged to meet all the men in public, the single women also often chose to be interviewed in public places; we met in restaurants or coffee shops.

In addition to the structured interviews, I conducted ongoing informal interviews. Although it is difficult to say how many informal conversations I had with attendees, I can say confidently that at some point I interacted with everybody in the congregation. Because of time constraints, some of these conversations never went beyond the basic introductions. (Among Messianics, introductions invariably include information on whether they are Jewish or Gentile, how long they have been Believers, and how long they have had a "Messianic vision.") Many conversations took place over invitations to lunch after services, in the parking lot after an event, at social Adat haRuach functions, or over the telephone.

At the beginning of my fieldwork, I was left to make contacts on my own. By the time Rabbi Jason officially introduced me to the congregation, I had already met most of the congregants and everyone knew who I was. In Rabbi Jason's introduction, he explained who I was and added that I had been "coming [to Shabbat services] for many months now and was very open about not being a Messianic Jew." Becky, his wife, added that I showed up with my yellow legal pad at every single congregation-related function and attended more events than even she did. Mike Pierce endorsed Rabbi Jason's support and told the congregants not to be frightened or wary of me; in my months there, he and his family had "grown to love me." I was pleased by his statements, but I later heard that some of the congregants found them troublesome and inappropriate.

I also felt that I was a part of the congregation when people called me on separate occasions, after I had moved back to Santa Barbara, to tell me that one congregant was sick (would I please pray for her?) and that another had died. I felt truly included when one of the congregants asked me to be a bridesmaid in her wedding. (I was the only non-Believer in the wedding party.)

Initially I had to make an effort to separate my worldview from those of the people I met. By the end of my fieldwork, however, I could appreciate what my respondents found in their religious expression. Like Davidman (1991), in her study of Orthodox women, I emerged from the study with greater empathy for the Messianic Jewish world, and with an increased interest in finding ways to express my own Jewish identity.

The only exception was my intolerance toward aggressive proselytizing (see chapter 3). The first encounter of this type occurred about a month into my fieldwork, when I brought my sister to an Adat haRuach function. A woman I did not know at the time approached us and asked if we were "completed Jews." I had prepared my sister for a range of responses and had explained various terms used by the Messianic community that she might find unfamiliar, but I had forgotten to inform her about this particular phrase. Unaware of the implications of "completed Jew," my sister answered, "Of course." The expressions *completed Jew* or *fulfilled Jew* are controversial even among Messianics. Some Believers find them offensive, but many take them to mean that their relationship with Yshua has made them *more* Jewish, or a "complete" Jew. My sister, unaware of this, understood the questioner to be asking whether she was completely Jewish. As she explained to the woman, both of our parents are Jewish; therefore she considers herself a "complete" Jew. I tried to explain to my sister that in Messianic terms we were not complete, and for the next forty minutes the woman told us why we should be.

I relayed this story, and my discomfort, to the Messianic couple who had driven us to the function, and the word spread. I did not realize that my distaste for "in-your-face" proselytization was becoming known in the congregation, but a few months later, when a member of the Outreach Committee aggressively witnessed to me, congregants (including some people who had not seen the interaction) apologized to me for days after the incident.

Not only were many congregants careful not to proselytize me openly; they also took care of me, as exemplified by a statement made to me near the end of my time at Adat haRuach. A woman I had come to know through the Women's Ministry said that she had kept an eye out for me throughout my time with the congregation. When I gave her an inquisitive look, she said that she knew what "eagles" some congregants could be, and she did not want any of them "descending down on my Shoshanah."

The mechanism that I unconsciously used for maintaining distance is termed "empathic disagreement;" it is one way of marking the differences between the researcher and those being studied (Gordon 1987).[1] Perhaps because of my fears of being banned from doing further fieldwork at Adat haRuach, or perhaps because of my distaste for confrontation, I did not openly disagree with congregants.[2] I felt that such disagreeing, or engaging in an argument, would be less fruitful than probing them on their beliefs. On the other hand, subtle signs of my own beliefs and disbeliefs must have been evident in the kinds of questions I asked and the underlying assumptions I made. This was made clear to me, soon after election time, when we were discussing the issues that had been on the ballot. A highly active Adat haRuach member turned to me and remarked laughingly, "But you probably voted like a bleeding-hearted liberal."

I was comfortable participating in the group; and I found that participation was a way to test the group's boundaries. Had I sat outside and merely watched, the congregants might have interpreted my nonparticipation as evidence that I had a "hardened heart." By being actively involved when I could, I (often inadvertently) gave clues as to where I stood. Again, I was not aware of this (I felt my way around a lot) until I commented to my neighbor at a service that I thought a Hebrew song particularly pretty and asked why we hadn't sung it before. She answered that we had sung it several weeks ago; didn't I remember? After all, she added, I had even sung the verses that mentioned Yshua. As she spoke, her big smile told me that congregants were aware not only of what I did or did not do, but of what verses of a song I sang.

The aspect of community life that receives a particularly large share of my attention is what Traweek (1988) terms "ecology,"—the environment that supports the group under study.[3] In situating Messianic Judaism in the North American religious landscape, I spent a substantial amount of time talking to leaders of the traditional Jewish community. These leaders were the regional/local directors of national organizations that deal with domestic Jewish issues: The American Jewish Committee, the American Jewish Congress, the Anti-Defamation League of B'nai B'rith, the Community Relations Committee of the Jewish Federation Council, the Simon Wiesenthal Center, the Cult Clinic under Jewish Family Services, Jewish Community Relations Council's Commission on Cults and Missionaries, and Jews for Judaism. The issues I discussed with them include the maintenance, propagation, and understanding of Jewish identity and Jewish culture, but not Israel/Zionism, religion (i.e., Torah, rabbis, cantors), or past events.

I limited my interviews in the traditional Jewish community to the Los Angeles area, home of the second-largest Jewish community in the United States and catering, like Adat haRuach, to Jews on the West Coast. I conducted most of these interviews in the representative's offices; two meetings were held in restaurants. The meetings ranged from one to four hours in length, although one relationship continued to the point where I was asked to (and did) audit for one semester a course on the Jewish community at the Los Angeles campus of Hebrew Union College.

Interview Guide for
Adat haRuach Congregants

I. Personal History/Biography

I'd like to start by asking you some questions about yourself.
>How old are you?
>Are you now, or have you ever been, married?
>Do you have children?
>How many?
>Do you work?
>Doing what?

I'm interested in knowing about your life before you became involved in Adat haRuach.
>Where did you grow up?
>What kind of home (Gentile/Jewish) did you grow up in?
>Was it a religious home?
>When (i.e., age, marital status at the time) did you become a Believer?
>How? What was going on in your life at that time?
>Are any of your family members Believers?
>How did they take your knowing the Lord?
>What's your relationship with them now?
>How did your friends at the time react?
>Do you see any of them now?

I'd like you to think about your five closest friends. Do any of them belong to Adat haRuach? Are any of them non-Believers?

II. Involvement/Participation

Tell me about your involvement in Adat haRuach.
>   When did you start attending services/functions?
>   Have you ever been to another Messianic congregation?
>   Why did you pick Adat haRuach in particular?
>   Are you a member?
>   Are you involved in any ministry?

What related activities do you participate in? (e.g., *havorah*, Bible study, Singles). How many hours a week/month do you spend doing Adat haRuach-related activities?

Do you participate in any other congregation?
>   If so, which?
>   How often?

So far, I get the sense that everybody celebrates holidays differently. I'm wondering, for example, if you celebrate Christmas and/or Easter. How?
>   Thanksgiving?
>   Halloween?
>   Do you observe Shabbat? How?
>   Do you keep kosher? How?

Could you explain to me why everybody does these things differently? (i.e., why do some people celebrate Christmas, others do not, and others keep kosher?)

Do you celebrate any of these holidays with your family? (Gentiles: Christmas/Easter; Jews: Shabbat/Passover) Is it problematic?

III. Attitudes

Secular World
I'd like to know a little about your feelings towards secular-world activities. How do feel about (how often do you do, listen to, etc.):

Movies (R-rated)
Books
Television
Radio/music
Newspapers
Secular education
Alcohol
Tobacco

Is this different from your life pre-Adat haRuach?

Family
I'd like to get a better understanding of your values and experiences concerning family life. What would you say the roles of mother/father, husband/wife are in the family?

What do you think are the most important issues for women in the Messianic movement?

Has the women's movement of the past twenty years had any impact on the Messianic movement? On men?

What do you believe is the ideal role for a Messianic woman in today's world?

Has your image of womanhood/manhood stayed the same or changed since your involvement in Adat haRuach?

Have your friendships changed since you came to Adat haRuach? Your relationships with members of the opposite sex? (If no: Have they changed since you became a Believer?)

Has your family life changed as a result of attending a Messianic congregation? (If not married: Has attending a congregation changed your expectations and goals regarding family life?)

Have your career plans changed since your involvement in Adat haRuach?

IV. Identity

If Gentile:
What was your interest in Judaism before you joined Adat haRuach?

Have you ever considered conversion to Judaism?

If Jewish:
Are there any parts of your Jewish identity or experience that you feel you had to compromise when you became a Believer?

Were you apprehensive when you first started attending services/functions at Adat haRuach?

What was the most important thing you learned about being Jewish at Adat haRuach?

What does being Jewish mean to you now?

What did it mean before?

If married:
How long have you been married?

Did you meet as Believers?

Do you have children? If yes, how many? What are their ages? Where do they go to school? (If they are homeschooled, why?)

If single:
What is it like to be single at Adat haRuach?

Would you like to be married?

To have a family?

Is it important to you that your spouse be Jewish/Gentile?

V. General Questions

What do you like most about the Messianic way of life? Least?

What are your plans and goals for the future? Have they changed or stayed the same since your involvement at Adat haRuach?

Are there any other ways in which becoming a Messianic has affected your life?

Is there any thing else you think I should know?

Any suggestions as to whom else I should speak to?

Interview Guide for Jewish Organizations

I'd like to start by asking you about your conception of the Jewish community in the United States. How might you define it?

What/who does the Jewish community include or exclude?

What do you see as the biggest threat to the integrity of the Jewish community in the United States?

Would you say that it is part of the general process of acculturation? How?

In your opinion, is conversion or intermarriage a bigger threat to the Jewish community? Why?

Does the relative threat depend on the type of religion the Jew converts to? (i.e., do some religions pose a larger threat?)

Do Jewish Christians (such as Messianic Jews, those who claim to be simultaneously Christian and Jewish) represent a threat to the Jewish community? In what way?

More or less so than Jews who convert and cease to identify as Jews?

More or less so than Jews who join "cults" and cease to identify as Jews?

Have any of the threats we've discussed changed over the years? For example, did the evangelizing campaign Key73 have any impact?

What about events dealing with Israel, such as the Six-Day War?

I have a sense that the memory of the Holocaust has influenced certain issues. Do you think its memory has affected what the community sees as a threat?

Does your organization deal actively with any of these issues?

How would you rate the efforts of the Jewish community in responding to these threats?

Who (else) do you think deals with these issues effectively?

Is there anything else you think I should know?

Do you have any suggestions about others to whom I should speak?

Notes

Chapter 1: Exodus and Communion

1. This chapter is based on participant observation and is supplemented by information presented by Fuchs (1985), Kasdan (1993), Liberman (1976), and Zimmerman (1981).

2. I have fictionalized Adat haRuach's name and location. Appendix A provides the rationale for fictionalizing the congregation's name, its location, and the identities of the adherents.

3. Many Adat haRuach congregants brought along family members in the hope that these relatives—Jews and Gentiles—would come to understand Messianic Judaism better and perhaps even join the congregants in their belief. Also among the invited were friends of congregants and a group of Jewish immigrants recently arrived from Russia, with their interpreter.

4. This is a reference to *bikkur chametz*, the yearly ritual of thoroughly inspecting one's home for any leavening.

5. The Messianic movement is made up of individuals who are ethnic Jews and Gentiles; I refer to them as Messianic Jews and Messianic Gentiles, respectively. When talking about both Gentiles and Jews, I use the term Messianic Believers to include all. When discussing the organized movement, however, I use the official name, Messianic Judaism.

6. McGuire (1982) refers to this movement as Pentecostal Catholicism. While Pentecostal Catholicism and Charismatic Catholicism are synonymous terms, I use the latter to describe the movement (see Burgess and McGee 1988).

7. There are scholarly debates about the definition of *Evangelical*. I use the term to mean those who take the Bible literally, are born again, and who encourage others to be saved while at the same time accomodate themselves to the ways of the modern world (Ammerman 1987:6–7). In talking about the "Jewish parent community," which I sometimes refer to as "mainstream," "mainline," or

"normative" Judaism, I mean the organized Jewish community which typically includes the three largest branches of Judaism—Reform, Conservative, and Orthodox Jewry. In other words, the traditional, inherited, normative, or median style of Jewish religion (Marty 1976).

Chapter 2: Boundaries, Threats, and Assimilation

1. For a better understanding of Jews for Jesus, see LaMagdeleine 1977 and Lipson 1990.

2. The Jewish community representatives are spokespeople for their representative organizations, so I have retained their real names. These interviews were conducted in 1992, and some of the spokespeople no longer work for, or represent, their respective organizations.

3. According to Mary Douglas (1970), societies can be divided into the grouplike and the gridlike. The group refers to the boundary that people erect between themselves and the outside world; the grid refers to the rules that govern interaction between individuals. Group, emphasizing the well-bounded quality of group life, represents a more corporate order than grid, which pertains more to collectivities of partial interests linked together. Old World Jewry is a typical strong group-oriented society, according to Douglas's typology. Members of that community stayed together largely because of the boundary between themselves and the rest of society, maintained by persecution and anti-Semitism.

4. See Markowitz (1993) for a discussion of the biological inalterability of Jewish identity among contemporary Russian/Soviet Jews.

5. For a more fully detailed account of the Christian religious product business (including bumper stickers), see *The New York Times* (1973c).

6. Anticult activities intensified after this mass suicide (Melton 1991, personal communication).

7. NRMs use Holocaust imagery as well (see Dujardin 1979; Hecht 1985; Kollin 1979; Rudin and Rudin 1980; Zeitlin 1984).

8. See Appel 1983; Barker 1984; Danzger 1989; Goldman 1990; Judah 1974; Richardson 1980; Rochford 1985; Stark and Bainbridge 1985; Tipton 1982.

9. Jewish anticult groups are not specific to North America, In Israel, the most effective anticult organization is a religious group involved in converting Jews to a religious perspective. It tries to substitute Orthodox Judaism for the new religious movements (Zaidman-Dvir et al. 1992).

Chapter 3: The History of Messianic Judaism

1. Most of the present congregations are in the United States, but *The Messianic Times* (1992b) claims that there are thirty-five active Messianic congregations in Israel, with three to five thousand Believers. In 1997, according to Zev Isaacs, managing editor of *The Messianic Times*, these figures have increased to one hundred Messianic congregations and fellowships and between five and ten thousand Messianic Believers in Israel (personal communication).

2. These terms are all very fluid and dynamic. Their meanings have changed throughout time and vary across individuals.

3. Jews for Jesus, a breakaway group from the ABMJ, is perhaps the most vocal and most aggressive of Jewish Christian groups. For detailed accounts of Jews for Jesus and their relationship to Jewish Christianity, see LaMagdeleine (1977) and Lipson (1990).

4. Dashefsky and Shapiro (1974) refer to this as "Jewish identification" (as opposed to Jewish "identity"). Gans (1956) has written that Judaization is when Judaism as a religion declines and the cultural tradition of Judaism is the tie that binds the Jewish community.

5. It is unclear to me whether the UMJC or the MJAA refer to themselves as a denomination. I use the term to mean an organization (regional, national, or international) that trains, certifies, disciplines, nurtures, provides leadership and financial support, and defines doctrine (Warner 1994).

6. The often-quoted number of 150,00 to 300,000 refers to the number of Jews who believe in Jesus but are not necessarily Messianic Jews (Kasdan 1997; Isaacs 1997).

7. It was Orthodox Judaism that responded most aggressively, precisely because it stresses boundaries. However, Messianic Judaism, as will become clearer in the next chapters, also stresses such boundaries.

8. Among Gentiles, being "Jewish" means being "Jewish-like" and/or worshipping in a "Jewish manner."

9. This is an increase from the 135 reported in 1992 (*The Messianic Times* 1992c, 1992d).

10. Although I have not fictionalized any of the situations I describe, in some cases I have changed the identities of the persons involved in those events. I did this to ensure their anonymity in the Adat haRuach community and in the Messianic community at large. In addition, I fictionalized the names of all the congregants because it was a condition of my entering the community. I did so even though some congregants expressed a desire to keep their real names, which created an ethical dilemma for me.

11. Bernstein (1997) and Isaacs (1997, personal communication) observe that, on average, congregations are made up of 50 percent Jews and 50 percent Gentiles.

12. This finding is quite consistent with that of Harris-Shapiro (1992), who also found that most Messianic adherents had been saved previously.

13. The term *Siddur* derives from an Old Hebrew word for "order" or "arrangement," which ironically emphasizes the traditional lack of flexibility in the order of the prayers. Individual prayers are not encouraged at any time or place.

14. My experience among Messianic Jews was very different, and seemingly easier, than that of Carol Harris-Shapiro (1992). Perhaps because of her standing as a rabbi, she was thought to represent the "establishment" and therefore was a constant reminder of the tensions between the normative and the Messianic Jewish communities. For whatever reason, her initial relations with congregation members were strained.

15. Warner (1988) and Neitz (1987) also tell how the congregants of the groups they studied felt that their congregation attended to their needs.

16. Unfortunately, exit interviewing of former members was beyond the scope of my study. These findings, however, suggest that the emotional investment demanded of Adat haRuach members is too high, at least for some, to sustain for a long time.

Chapter 4: "*Meshuganeh* for the Lord"

1. The biblical passage quoted as support of this stance is 1 Corinthians 7:17–20, in which Paul states that all should remain as they were when called to God.

2. At the time, services at Adat haRuach were held Friday nights, rather than on Saturday mornings, as is the custom now. "Coming to the Lord" at the same time as a spouse was not a common narrative in my field experience. It is something that was considered a special bond, but it did not occur among most couples I spoke to.

3. These findings echo those of Jacobs (1996). In her work on crypto-Jews in the southwest United States, she found men and women who engaged in the process of recovering their Sephardic roots who wished to revive a connection to their Jewish heritage.

4. See also Jacobs (1996) for a discussion of how crypto-Jews reconstruct evidence for Sephardic ancestry based on dietary customs relating to *kashrut* (Hebrew for "ritually pure"; used to refer to (kosher) dietary laws.

5. Both Liliana and Thomas use the term *Marrano* to describe their ancestors. *Marrano, Converso,* and *Anusim* are terms used for those Jews who ostensibly became Christian but remained secret Jews as a result of the Inquisition. The term preferred by contemporary scholars is crypto-Jew (Gitlitz 1996; Jacobs 1996).

6. Chillingly, this criterion was used by the Nazi regime to determine who was a Jew.

7. Shelly, for example, told me about the time she asked her father about their ancestry. Her Danish grandparents' name was Davidsen. Shelly hoped that this reflected a Jewish background, but could not uncover any Jewish connection. Her father still asks her teasingly, "You want to know about the Davidsteins?"

Chapter 5: Community Building

1. According to Douglas (1970, 40), Antiochus "forced into prominence the rule concerning pork as the cultural symbol of group allegiance." It is a symbol of allegiance simply because it lacks meaning for other cultures.

2. See Neitz (1987) for another account of how new religious organizations view parent organizations as lacking in spirituality.

3. This is unlike mainline Jews who, if they keep kosher, generally adhere to rabbinic kosher law. However, the extent to which biblical *kashrut* is practiced among mainline Jews is not entirely clear.

4. For them, keeping kosher is a way of being identified with Judaism without the support of organizational or culture structures of Jewish culture. For more detail on symbolic ethnicity, see Alba 1990; Gans 1979, 1994; Waters 1990.

5. Sara's mother reported to me that her new faith was less offensive to her and the rest of their Jewish family than Sara's new understanding of certain political issues. Sara's parents were one of the few parents of congregants I met during my time at Adat haRuach. It is unfortunate I did not meet more, since it would be interesting to look—from the parents' perspective—at the break that occurs between Messianic Believers and their parents.

6. A reference to the taboo in Judaism on saying God's name.

Chapter 6: "The Only Thing I Do at Easter Is Passover"

1. Messianic Judaism has found a way to blend the Jewish and Christian calendars. Yet, according to Zerubavel, the symbiosis of two groups with two different ritual calendars is impossible because the calendar "contributes to the establishment of intergroup boundaries that distinguish, as well as separate, group members from "outsiders" (1982: 288).

2. Some congregations hold services on Fridays and/or Saturdays (see Harris-Shapiro 1992; Kohn 1985).

3. To understand what Shabbat observance is like for individual Messianic Believers, I examined the responses of nineteen family units—ten single

respondents and nine couples—to the question "Do you observe Shabbat?" Eleven answered "yes," and eight answered "no" or "not really."

4. Of the eight who said they did not observe Shabbat, seven were single. In contrast, of the eleven who categorized themselves as observers, only three were single. Couples were more likely than singles to "do both" (lighting candles and not working). For instance, six of seven households that both lit candles and avoided working were married. In contrast, only two of the ten singles both lit candles and avoided working.

5. When her mother does not join them, Ilana adds "*V'nantan lanu Y'shua h'aorleh olam*" ("who has given us Yshua, the light of the world") to the blessings.

6. Purim is another non-Biblical celebration observed by Messianic Believers and Orthodox Jews. While Jewish children dress up almost exclusively as historically relevant figures, the Messianic Believers' Purim costumes I have seen include a "Yshua Freak" (a tongue-in-cheek reference to Jesus Freaks), and a Hasidic family. My personal favorite was two small boys who were dressed up as a strawberry and an apple to denote the New Testament quote, "be fruitful and multiply."

7. From the Jewish New Testament (Stern 1989), "Then came Hanukkah in Yerushalayim. It was winter and Yeshua was walking around inside the Temple area, in Shlomo's Colonnade."

8. Five of the six Gentile family units celebrated Christmas in some way, but two-thirds of the Root-seeker and intermarried family units, and only one-third of ethnic Jews, did so. Furthermore, half of all Gentiles initiated the celebration of Christmas in their own homes, but none of the ethnic Jews did so.

9. The distinction between observance and nonobservance among singles versus couples that I noted with regard to Shabbat celebration does not seem to hold true of Christmas celebration. Of the eleven congregants who celebrate Christmas, seven are single. In contrast, of the seven who do not celebrate Christmas, three were single and the other four are married couples.

10. In other religious organizations, the Devil is the mobilizing factor that all rally around to oppose (Ammerman 1987).

11. For a comprehensive description of the feasts, see Fischer (1983); Kasdan (1993); Liberman (1976); Schiffman (1992); and Zimmerman (1981).

12. For example, Messianics believe that according to the New Testament some of these feasts were fulfilled by Yshua, who did not abolish or set aside the Law and its teachings but gave them added significance (Fischer 1983). Among Messianic Believers, it is understood that the three spring feasts were fulfilled at the first coming—Yshua was crucified on Passover and rose three days later on Sfirat Haomer (the Early First Fruits); and the Holy Spirit was poured out on Shavuot (Pentecost or the Latter First Fruits). The autumn holy days represent those feasts that have not yet been fulfilled. These are Rosh Hashanah,

representing the rapture; Yom Kippur, symbolizing Judgment; and Sukkot, representing Jesus's reign as Messiah. These will not be fulfilled until the second coming (see also Kasdan 1993).

13. Likewise, Charasmatic Catholics add Catholic ritual to the experiential religious expression, but it is a reinterpreted ritual that they believe contributes to their new religious identity. These are not necessary for one's spiritual life, but they enrich one's relationship with God (Neitz 1987).

Chapter 7: Bringing Home the Bacon

1. *Shamishim*, or deacons, are available for helping with spiritual or practical needs. At the time of my fieldwork, three men filled this role at Adat haRuach. In late 1997, the number of *shamishim* had increased to nine, five of whom are women.

2. Messianic marriage is strongly patrilocal: If a Messianic woman marries a Gentile man, she is expected to follow him to his church. This is also the practice among Evangelical Christians, but it contrasts sharply with Orthodox Jewish custom, in which the home and the children are Jewish only if the woman is Jewish. If the husband's and the wife's families follow different dietary laws (Ashkenazic versus Sephardic, for example), the new household follows the custom of the wife's family.

3. A couple can be divorced only if one spouse commits adultery, or if one is not a Believer and leaves the other. In either case, the injured party is obliged to forgive and ask the spouse to resume the marriage (on the basis of 1 Corinthians 7). One becomes biblically free only if the spouse does not respond.

4. One unmarried respondent felt that this distinction was true of marital status as well; he feels that he is left out of events because he is single.

5. Personal communication with God for this purpose is foreign to traditional Jewish theology since a "personal relationship" with God is not part of the religious belief system. If Jews seek approval for nontraditional arrangements, they consult the community's rabbi (or other authority).

Chapter 8: Looking toward the Future

1. This point is in keeping with Roof and McKinney's work on conservative Protestantism. They comment that Americans change religious affiliation easily, and that,

The religious individualism of modern America encourages sifting and sorting on the basis of shifting perceptions. . . . Individual preferences in matters of faith operate more freely; believers are less bound by the strictures of group belonging, by custom and tradition. As conformity in religious life has declined, choice has become a more important factor. (1988:181)

Appendix A

1. In his own work with Jesus People groups, Gordon found that research relationships with proselytizing groups are maintained successfully only when the field researcher helps the group to define the situation. If this is not done, he points out, the researchers feel "subjective distress," which includes fear, discomfort, annoyance, and guilt with regard to the group.

2. Gordon (1987) advocates open discussion of the researcher's beliefs, and cites Richardson et al.'s (1979) open discussion of their beliefs and disagreements with the Jesus People they studied.

3. In her ethnography of physicists, anthropologist Sharon Traweek (1988) delineates four aspects of community life that an ethnographic account should address: ecology, or the environment that supports the group; social organization, or how the group structures itself; the developmental cycle, or how the group passes on its values to the next generation; and cosmology—the group's system of knowledge, including what is valued or denigrated. I attempted to incorporate all four of these domains into this work. Yet because these categories are somewhat artificial, I have not divided the work neatly into these four sections. Instead I address the domains as part of a larger whole.

References Cited

Alba, Richard D.
    1990 *Ethnic Identity: The Transformation of White America.* New Haven:
    Yale University Press.

Aidala, Angela
    1985 "Social Change, Gender Roles, and New Religious Movements."
    Sociological Analysis 46(3):287–314.

American Jewish Committee Memorandum
    1972 "Some Issues Raised by Forthcoming Evangelism Campaigns: A
    Background Memorandum," by Rabbi Marc Tanenbaum, June, 1–13.
    New York: American Jewish Committee.

Ammerman, Nancy Tatom
    1987 *Bible Believers: Fundamentalists in the Modern World.* New
    Brunswick: Rutgers University Press.
    1992 "Submit to Your Husbands as to the Lord: The Ambiguities of Gender
    and Power in Christian Fundamentalism." Paper presented at the annual
    meeting of the Association for the Sociology of Religion/American
    Sociological Association, Pittsburgh, August.

Appel, Willa
    1983 *Cults in America: Programmed for Paradise.* New York: Holt, Rinehart
    and Winston.

Aviad, Janet O'Dea
    1983 *Return to Judaism: Religious Renewal in Israel.* Chicago: University of
    Chicago Press.

Balmer, Randall Herbert
  1989 *Mine Eyes Have Seen the Glory: A Journey into the Evangelical Subculture in America.* New York: Oxford University Press.

Barker, Eileen
  1984 *The Making of a Moonie: Choice or Brainwashing?* Oxford: Basil Blackwell.

Barst, Irving Bernard
  1992 "A Jew's Testimony." *Pentecostal Evangel* (February 9, n.p.).

Barth, Fredrik
  1969 "Introduction." In *Ethnic Group and Boundaries: The Social Organization of Culture and Difference*, edited by Fredrik Barth, 9–38. Bergen, Norway: Universitetsforlaget; and London: Allen and Unwin.

Becker, Penny
  1994 "Mining the Tradition: Social Change and Culture Work in Two Religious Organizations." Paper presented at the annual meetings of the Society for the Scientific Study of Religion, Albuquerque.

Bernards, Solomon
  1973 "Key 73—A Jewish View." *Christian Century* 90(1):12–4.

Bernstein, Howard
  1997 "Evangelizing Jews: Messianic Jews Versus Jews for Jesus." Paper presented at the annual meeting of the Association for the Sociology of Religion, Toronto, August.

Bershtel, Sara and Allen Graubard
  1992 *Saving Remnants: Feeling Jewish in America.* New York: Free Press.

Brickner, Balfour
  1978 "Christian Missionaries and a Jewish Response." *Jewish Digest* 23 (Summer):10–19.

Burgess, Stanley M., and Gary B. McGee, eds.
  1988 *Dictionary of Pentecostal and Charistmatic Movements.* Grand Rapids, Mich.: Regency Reference Library.

Cannadine, David
    1983 "The Context, Performance and Meaning of Ritual: The British Monarchy and the "Invention of Tradition," c. 1820–1977." In *The Invention of Tradition*, edited by Eric Hobsbawm and Terence Ranger, 101–64. Cambridge: Cambridge University Press.

Christianity Today
    1988 "'Fulfilled' Jews or 'Former Jews'?" 32(14):66–8.

Danzger, M. Herbert
    1989 *Returning to Tradition: The Contemporary Revival of Orthodox Judaism*. New Haven: Yale University Press.

Dashefsky, Arnold, and Howard M. Shapiro
    1992 *Ethnic Identification among American Jews: Socialization and Social Structure*. Lanham, Md.: University Press of America.

Davidman, Lynn
    1991 *Tradition in a Rootless World: Women Turn to Orthodox Judaism*. Berkeley and Los Angeles: University of California Press.

Davidman, Lynn, and Arthur Greil L.
    1993 "Gender and the Experience of Conversion: The Case of 'Returnees' to Modern Orthodox Judaism." *Sociology of Religion* 54(1):83–100.

Dolgin, Janet L.
    1977 *Jewish Identity and the JDL*. Princeton: Princeton University Press.

Douglas, Mary
    1966 *Purity and Danger: An Analysis of Concepts of Pollution and Taboo*. New York: Frederick A. Praeger.
    1970 *Natural Symbols: Explorations in Cosmology*. New York: Pantheon Books.

Dujardin, Richard C.
    1979 *The Providence Journal*. Providence, R.I. (April 23.)

Eichhorn, David Max
    1978 *Evangelizing the American Jew*. Middle Village, N.Y.: Jonathan David.

Eiesland, Nancy L.
    1997 "A Strange Road Home: Adult Female Converts to Classical
    Pentecostalism." In *Mixed Blessings: Gender and Religious
    Fundamentalism Cross Culturally*, edited by Judy Brink and Joan
    Mencher, 91–115. New York and London: Routledge.

Elazar, Daniel Judah
    1976 *Community and Polity: The Organizational Dynamics of American
    Jewry*. Philadelphia: Jewish Publication Society of America.

Endelman, Todd M.
    1987 *Jewish Apostasy in the Modern World*. New York: Holmes and Meier.

Feher, Shoshanah
    1988 "From the Rivers of Babylon to the Valley of Los Angeles: The Exodus
    and Adaptation of Iranian Jews." In *Gatherings in Diaspora: Religious
    Communities and the New Immigration,"* edited by R. Stephen Warner
    and Judith G. Wittner, 71–94. Philadelphia: Temple University Press.

Fein, Leonard J.
    1988 *Where Are We?: The Inner Life of America's Jews*. New York: Harper
    and Row.

Fichter, Joseph
    1976 "Parallel Conversions: Charismatics and Recovered Alcoholics."
    Christian Century 93:148–50.

Finke, Roger, and Rodney Stark
    1992 *The Churching of America, 1776–1990: Winners and Losers in Our
    Religious Economy*. New Brunswick: Rutgers University Press.

Fischer, John
    1983 *The Olive Tree Connection*. Palm Harbor, Fla.: Menorah Ministries.

Fredriksen, Paula
    1988 *From Jesus to Christ: The Origins of the New Testament Images of
    Jesus*. New Haven: Yale University Press.

Fruchtenbaum, Arnold G.
1974 *Hebrew Christianity: Its Theology, History and Philosophy.*
Washington, D.C.: Canon Press.

Fuchs, Daniel
1985 *Israel's Holy Days: In Type and Prophecy.* Neptune, N.J.: Loizeaux
Brothers.

Gans, Herbert J.
1956 "American Jewry: Present and Future." *Commentary* 21(5):423–30.
1979 "Symbolic Ethnicity: The Future of Ethnic Groups and Cultures in
America." *Ethnic and Racial Studies* 2(1):1–20.
1994 "Symbolic Ethnicity and Symbolic Religiosity: Toward a Comparison
of Ethnic and Religious Acculturation." *Ethnic and Racial Studies*
17(4):577–92.

Gitlitz, David M.
1996 *Secrecy and Deceit: The Religion of the Crypto-Jews.* Philadelphia:
Jewish Publication Society of America.

Glazer, Nathan
1972 *American Judaism.* 2d ed. Chicago: University of Chicago Press.

Goffman, Erving
1959 *The Presentation of Self in Everyday Life.* Garden City, N.Y.:
Doubleday.
1963 *Stigma: Notes on the Management of Spoiled Identity.* Englewood
Cliffs, N.J.:Prentice-Hall.

Goldberg, Louis
1974 "The Messianic Jew." *Christianity Today,* (February 1, pp. [494]6–
[499]11).

Goldman, Marion
1990 "From Promiscuity to Celibacy: Sexual Regulation at Rajneeshpuram."
Paper presented at the annual meeting of the Society for the Scientific
Study of Religion, Virginia Beach, Va.

Goldscheider, Calvin, and Alan S. Zuckerman
    1984 *The Transformation of the Jews.* Chicago: University of Chicago Press.

Gordon, David F.
    1987 "Getting Close By Staying Distant: Fieldwork with Proselytizing
    Groups." *Qualitative Sociology* 10(3):267–87.

Gray, Edward R., and Scott L. Thumma
    1997 "The Gospel Hour: Liminality, Identity, and Religion in a Gay Bar." In
    Contemporary American Religion: An Ethnographic Reader, edited by
    Penny Edgell Becker and Nancy L. Eiesland, 79–98. Walnut Creek,
    Calif.: AltaMira Press.

Gusfield, Joseph R.
    1975 *Community: A Critical Response.* Oxford: Basil Blackwell.

Hall, John R.
    1988 "Social Organization and Pathways of Commitment: Types of
    Communal Groups, Rational Choice Theory, and the Kanter Thesis."
    American Sociological Review 53(5):679–92.

Harris-Shapiro, Carol A.
    1992 "Syncretism or Struggle: The Case of Messianic Judaism." Ph.D. diss.,
    Department of Religion, Temple University.

Heald, Cynthia
    1992 *Becoming a Woman of Excellence.* Colorado Springs: NavPress.

Hecht, Shea
    1985 *Confessions of a Jewish Cultbuster.* Brooklyn: Tosefos Media.

Heilman, Samuel
    1992 *Defenders of the Faith: Inside Ultra-Orthodox Jewry.* New York:
    Schocken.

Herman, Simon C.
    1970 *Israelis and Jews: The Continuity of an Identity.* New York: Random
    House.
    1989 *Jewish Identity: A Social Psychological Perspective.* New Brunswick,
    N.J.: Transaction.

Hirschman, Albert O.
  1970 *Exit, Voice, and Loyalty: Responses to Decline in Firms, Organizations, and States.* Cambridge: Harvard University Press.

Hobsbawm, Eric
  1983 "Introduction: Inventing Traditions." In *The Invention of Tradition,* edited by Eric Hobsbawm and Terence Ranger, 1–14. Cambridge: Cambridge University Press.

Isser, Natalie, and Lita Linzer Schwartz
  1980 "Community Responses to the Proselytization of Jews." *Journal of Jewish Communal Service* 57:63–72.

Jacobs, Janet Liebman
  1996 "Women, Ritual, and Secrecy: The Creation of Crypto-Jewish Culture." *Journal for the Scientific Study of Religion* 35(2):97–108.

Judah, J. Stillson
  1974 *Hare Krishna and the Counterculture.* New York: John Wiley and Sons.

Juster, Daniel C., with Daniel W. Pawley
  1981 "A Messianic Jew Pleads His Case." *Christianity Today* 26:7 [sic] (April 24:[587]22–[590]25).

Kasdan, Barney
  1993 *God's Appointed Times: A Practical Guide for Understanding and Celebrating the Biblical Holidays.* Baltimore: Lederer Messianic Publications.

Kaufman, Debra Renee
  1991 *Rachel's Daughters: Newly Orthodox Jewish Women.* New Brunswick: Rutgers University Press.

Kelley, Dean M.
  1972 *Why Conservative Churches Are Growing: A Study in the Sociology of Religion.* New York: Harper and Row.

Klatch, Rebecca E.
   1987 *Women of the New Right.* Philadelphia: Temple University Press.

Kohn, Rachel L. E.
   1985 "Hebrew Christianity and Messianic Judaism on the Church-Sect
      Continuum." Ph.D. diss., McMaster University, Department of Religious
      Studies.
   1987 "Ethnic Judaism and the Messianic Movement." *Jewish Journal of
      Sociology* 29(2):85–96.

Kollin, Gilbert
   1979 "Perversity." *Jewish Spectator* 44:61–2.

Kosmin, Barry A., Sidney Goldstein, Joseph Waksberg, Nava Lerer, Ariella
Keysar, and Jeffrey Scheckner
   1990 *Highlights of the CJF 1990 National Population Survey.* New York:
      Council of Jewish Federations.

Kosmin, Barry A., and Jeffrey Scheckner
   1992 "Jewish Population in the United States." In *American Jewish Year
      Book*, edited by David Singer and Ruth Seldin. Philadelphia: Jewish
      Publication Society of America.

Kurien, Prema
   1988 "Becoming American by Becoming Hindu: Indian Americans Take
      their Place at the Multi-Cultural Table. In *Gatherings in Diaspora:
      Religious Communities and the New Immigration,*" edited by R. Stephen
      Warner and Judith G. Wittner., 37–70. Philadelphia: Temple University
      Press.

LaMagdeleine, Donald
   1977 *Jews for Jesus: Organizational Structure and Supporters.* M.A. thesis,
      Graduate Theological Union.

Lawless, Elaine J.
   1988 *God's Peculiar People: Women's Voices and Folk Tradition in a
      Pentecostal Church.* Lexington: University Press of Kentucky.

Lawson, Matthew P.
1997 "Struggles for Mutual Reverence: Social Strategies and Religious Stories." In *Contemporary American Religion: An Ethnographic Reader,* edited by Penny Edgell Becker and Nancy L. Eiesland, 51–77. Walnut Creek: AltaMira Press.

Leonard, Karen Isaksen
1992 *Making Ethnic Choices: California's Punjabi Mexican Americans.* Philadelphia: Temple University Press.

Liberman, Paul.
1976 *The Fig Tree Blossoms: Messianic Judaism Emerges.* Indianola, Iowa: Fountain Press.

Lipset, Seymour Martin, ed.
1990 *American Pluralism and the Jewish Community.* New Brunswick, N.J.: Transaction.

Lipson, Juliene
1988 *Jews for Jesus: An Anthropological Study.* New York: AMS Press.

Maryland Baptist
1972a "Jewish, Christian, Theologians Discuss 'Civil Religion,'" by Mike Creswell. (November 23, n.p.)
1972b "Starke Answers Jewish Criticism of Key73," (March 15, n.p.)

Markowitz, Fran
1993 *A Community in Spite of Itself: Soviet Jewish Émigrés in New York.* Washington, D.C.: Smithsonian Institution.

Marty, Martin E.
1976 *A Nation of Behavers.* Chicago: University of Chicago Press.

McGuire, Meredith B.
1982 *Pentecostal Catholics: Power, Charisma, and Order in a Religious Movement.* Philadelphia: Temple University Press.

Medding, Peter, Gary Tobin, Sylvia Barack Fishman, and Mordechai Rimor
    1992 "Jewish Identity in Conversionary and Mixed Marriages." In *American
        Jewish Year Book*, edited by David Singer and Ruth Seldin, 3–76.
        Philadelphia: Jewish Publication Society of America.

Messianic Times
    1992a "Editorial: I Am Not Ashamed." (Winter, p. 4.)
    1992b "Letters to the Editor." (Winter, p. 4.)
    1992c "Colorado Jewish Newspaper Reviews the Messianic Times."
        (Winter, n.p.)
    1992d "Messianic Congregation and Organization Directory." (Winter, pp.
        17–8.)
    1992e "Advertisement: Kenmar Gifts." (Summer, p. 8.)

Methodist Reporter
    1973 "Rabbi Charges that Key73 'Validates' Radical Groups." (March
        23, p. 3.)

Miller, Donald E.
    1997 *Reinventing American Protestantism: Christianity in the New
        Millennium*. Berkeley and Los Angeles: University of California Press.

Mirsky, Norman B.
    1978 *Unorthodox Judaism*. Columbus: Ohio State University Press.

Moore, Deborah Dash
    1994 *To the Golden Cities: Pursuing the American Jewish Dream in Miami
        and Los Angeles*. New York: Free Press.

Morgan, Prys
    1983 "From a Death to a View: The Hunt for the Welsh Past in the Romantic
        Period." In *The Invention of Tradition*, edited by Eric Hobsbawm and
        Terence Ranger, 43–100. Cambridge: Cambridge University Press.

Nagel, Joane
    1994 "Constructing Ethnicity: Creating and Recreating Ethnic Identity and
        Culture." *Social Problems* 41(1):152–73.

Neitz, Mary Jo
    1987 *Charisma and Community: A Study of Religious Commitment within
        the Charismatic Renewal*. New Brunswick, N.J.: Transaction.

Neri, Judy
  1984 "Combatting Cults." *B'nai B'rith International Jewish Monthly* 98 (June/July):43–5.

Neusner, Jacob
  1981 *Stranger at Home: "The Holocaust," Zionism, and American Judaism.* Chicago: University of Chicago Press.

New York Baptist
  1973 "It Looks as though our Jewish Friends Are Giving Key73 the Lift-Off Thrust!" (February 15, p. 2.)

New York Times
  1973a "140 Church Group Join in Huge Evangelical Drive," by Eleanor Blau. (January 7, n.p.)
  1973b "Rabbi Questions Critiques of Key'73," by Edward Fiske. (January 28, p. 50.)
  1973c "Bible Bumper Stickers Big Business Over U.S." (February, 13 n.p.)
  1973d "Major Evangelical Drive Appears a Failure Over-All," by Eleanor Blau. (September 2, n.p.)

Newsweek
  1973 "Jews For Jesus" (March 19, p. 59.)

Nippert-Eng, Christena E.
  1996 *Home and Work: Negotiating Boundaries through Everyday Life.* Chicago: University of Chicago Press.

Ozorak, Elizabeth Weiss
  1996 "The Power, but Not the Glory: How Women Empower Themselves through Religion." *Journal for the Scientific Study of Religion* 35(1):17–29.

Perrin, Robin D., and Armand L. Mauss
  1991. "Saints and Seekers: Sources of Recruitment to the Vineyard Christian Fellowship." *Review of Religious Research* 33(2):97–111.

Pohli, Carol Virginia
  1983 "Church Closets and Back Doors: A Feminist View of Moral Majority Women." *Feminist Studies* 9(3):529–58.

Quebedeaux, Richard
    1978 *The Worldly Evangelicals*. San Francisco: Harper and Row.

Rausch, David A.
    1982a *Messianic Judaism: Its History, Theology and Polity*. Lewiston, N.Y.:
        Edwin Mellen Press.
    1982b "The Messianic Jewish Congregational Movement." *Christian
        Century*, September 15–22:926–9.

Richardson, James T.
    1986 "Jewish Participation in So-Called Cults: Spiritual Seduction or Active
        Agency?" Paper presented at the annual meetings of the Society for the
        Scientific Study of Religion, Washington, D.C., November.

Richardson, James T., Mary White Stewart, and Robert B. Simmonds
    1979 *Organized Miracles: A Study of a Contemporary, Youth, Communal,
        Fundamentalist Organization*. New Brunswick, N.J.: Transaction.

Rochford, Burke
    1985 *Hare Krishna in America*. New Brunswick: Rutgers University Press.

Roof, Wade Clark
    1993 *A Generation of Seekers: The Spiritual Journeys of the Baby Boom
        Generation*. San Francisco: Harper.

Roof, Wade Clark, and William McKinney.
    1988 *American Mainline Religion: Its Changing Shape and Future*. New
        Brunswick: Rutgers University Press.

Rose, Susan D.
    1987 "Women Warriors: The Negotiation of Gender in a Charismatic
        Community." *Sociological Analysis* 48(3):245–58.

Rottenberg, Isaac C.
    1992 "Messianic Jews: A Troubling Presence." *First Things* 28
        (December):26–32.

Royce, Anya Peterson
    1982 *Ethnic Identity: Strategies of Diversity*. Bloomington: Indiana
        University Press.

Rudin, A. James, and Marcia R. Rudin
1980 *Prison or Paradise?: The New Religious Cults.* Philadelphia: Fortress Sage.

Schiffman, Michael
1992 *The Return of the Remnant: The Rebirth of Messianic Judaism.* Baltimore: Lederer Publications.

Schnapper, Dominique
1983 *Jewish Identities in France: An Analysis of Contemporary French Jewry,* translated by Arthur Goldhammer. Chicago: University of Chicago Press.

Schonfield, Hugh
1936 *The History of Jewish Christianity: From the First to the Twentieth Century.* London: Duckworth.

Schwartz, Alan M.
1982 "Watch Out for The Way." *ADL Bulletin* 39:11–3.

Shibutani, Tamotsu and Kian M. Kwan
1965 *Ethnic Stratification: A Comparative Approach.* New York: MacMillan.

Sidey, Ken
1990 "Messianic Jews Seek Visibility, Respect." *Christianity Today* 43(9):72.

Sobel, B. Zvi
1974 *Hebrew Christianity: The Thirteenth Tribe.* New York: John Wiley and Sons.

Spalding, Henry D., ed.
1969 *Encyclopedia of Jewish Humor: From Biblical Times to the Modern Age.* New York: Jonathan David Publishers.

Stacey, Judith
1983 "The New Conservative Feminism." *Feminist Studies* 9(3):559–83.
1987 "Sexism by a Subtler Name?: Postindustrial Conditions and Postfeminist Consciousness in the Silicon Valley." *Socialist Review* 17(6):7–28.

1990 *Brave New Families: Stories of Domestic Upheaval in Late Twentieth Century America.* New York: Basic Books.

Stacey, Judith, and Susan Elizabeth Gerard
1990 "'We Are Not Doormats': The Influence of Feminism on Contemporary Evangelicals in the United States." In *Uncertain Terms: Negotiating Gender in American Culture*, edited by Faye Ginsberg and Anna Lowenhaupt Tsing, 98–117. Boston: Beacon Press.

The Star
1973 "Describes Conversion Drive Aimed at Some Jews," by Phyllis Feuerstein (February 1, pp. 2–11.)

Stark, Rodney
1987 "How New Religions Succeed: A Theoretical Model." In *The Future of New Religious Movements*, edited by Phillip E. Hammond and David G. Bromley, 11–29. Macon, Georgia: Mercer University Press.

Stark, Rodney, and William Simms Bainbridge
1985 *The Future of Religion: Secularization, Revival, and Cult Formation.* Berkeley and Los Angeles: University of California Press.

Stern, David
1988 *The Jewish Manifesto.* Clarksville, Md., and Jerusalem: Jewish New Testament Publications.
1989 *Jewish New Testament.* Clarksville, Md., and Jerusalem: Jewish New Testament Publications.

Stocks, Janet
1997 "To Stay or to Leave? Organizational Legitimacy in the Struggle for Change among Evangelical Feminists." In *Contemporary American Religion: An Ethnographic Reader*, edited by Penny Edgell Becker and Nancy L. Eiesland, 99–119. Walnut Creek, Calif.: AltaMira Press

Stokes, Bruce H.
1994 "Messianic Judaism: Ethnicity in Revitalization." Ph.D. diss., Department of Anthropology, University of California, Riverside.

Street'n Steeple
1972 "Evangelism Actions of General Conference." 6(3):1–2.

Swidler, Ann
    1986 "Culture in Action: Symbols and Strategies." *American Sociological Review* 51:273–86.

Texas Methodist
    1972 "Christian Evangelism Blasted." (December 22, n.p.)
    1973a "Key73 Head Responds to Jews." (January 26, n.p.)
    1973b "Billy Graham Clarifies Key73 Jewish Stance." (March 16, n.p.)
    1973c "Key73 Originator Denounces 'Wolfcries' Against Evangelism." (April 20, n.p.)

Thumma, Scott
    1991 "Negotiating a Religious Identity: The Case of the Gay Evangelical." *Sociological Analysis* 52(4):333–47.

Tipton, Steve
    Getting Saved from the Sixties: Moral Meaning in Conversion and Cultural Change. Berkeley and Los Angeles: University of California Press.

Traweek, Sharon
    1988 *Beamtimes and Lifetimes: The World of High Energy Physicists*. Cambridge: Harvard University Press.

Turner, Victor Witter
    1987 "Betwixt and Between: The Liminal Period in the Rites of Passage." In *Betwixt & Between: Patterns of Masculine and Feminine Initiation*, edited by Louise Caurs Mahdi, Steven Foster, and Meredith Little, 3–19. LaSalle, Illinois: Open Court.
    1977 [1969] *The Ritual Process: Structure and Anti-Structure*. Ithaca: Cornell University Press.

United Methodist Reporter
    1973a "Key73 Inertia Cited by Pastor, Rabbi on Panel." (May 18, n.p.)
    1973b "Rabbi Sees Key73 as '73 Challenge to Judaism," (August 24, n.p.)

Warner, R. Stephen
    1988 *New Wine in Old Wineskins*. Berkeley and Los Angeles: University of California Press.
    1994 "The Place of the Congregation in the Contemporary American

Religious Configuration." In *American Congregations*, edited by James P. Wind and James W. Lewis, volume 2, 54–99. Chicago: University of Chicago Press.

Warner, R. Stephen, and Judith G. Wittner, eds.
1998 *Gatherings in Diaspora: Religious Communities and the New Immigration.* Philadelphia: Temple University Press, (in press).

Waters, Mary C.
1990 *Ethnic Options: Choosing Identities in America.* Berkeley and Los Angeles: University of California Press.

Weigert, Andrew J., J. Smith Teitge, and Dennis W. Teitge
1986 *Society and Identity: Toward a Sociological Psychology.* Cambridge: Cambridge University Press.

Western Recorder
1973a "Key73 Negates Jews' Relationship to God, Rabbi Says," (April 7, p. 11.)
1973b "Nature of Evangelism is Key73 Problem—Tanenbaum." (April 7, p. 11.)
1973c "Jewish Criticism of Key73 Answered." (March 3, p. 6.)

Wiesel, Elie
1988 "The Missionary Menace." In *Smashing the Idols: A Jewish Inquiry into the Cult Phenomenon*, edited by Gary D. Eisenberg, 161–3. Northvale, N.J.: Jason Aronson.

Wirth, Louis
1956 [1928] *The Ghetto.* Chicago: University of Chicago Press.

Zaidman-Dvir, Nurit, and Stephen Sharot
1992 "The Response of Israeli Society to New Religious Movements: ISKCON and Teshuvah." *Journal for the Scientific Study of Religion* 31(3):279–95.

Zborowski, Mark, and Elizabeth Herzog
1974 *Life Is with People: The Culture of the Shtetl.* New York: Schocken.

Zeitlin, Marianne Langer
1984 "Regaining a Child from a Cult." *Jewish Digest* 29:3–5.

Zerubavel, Eviatar
1982 "Easter and Passover: On Calendars and Group Identity." *American Sociological Review* 47(2):284–9.
1991 *The Fine Line: Making Distinctions in Everyday Life.* New York: Free Press.

Zimmerman, Martha
1981 *Celebrate the Feasts of the Old Testament in your Own Home or Church.* Minneapolis: Bethany House Publishers.

Index

Page numbers enclosed in parentheses indicate the page on which the text of an endnote appears.

G

Authors Cited

Page numbers enclosed in parentheses indicate the page on
an endnote appears.